DATE DUE

MAY 31 08			
JAN 0 2 2010			

ARCHIT E
A T
A Rou

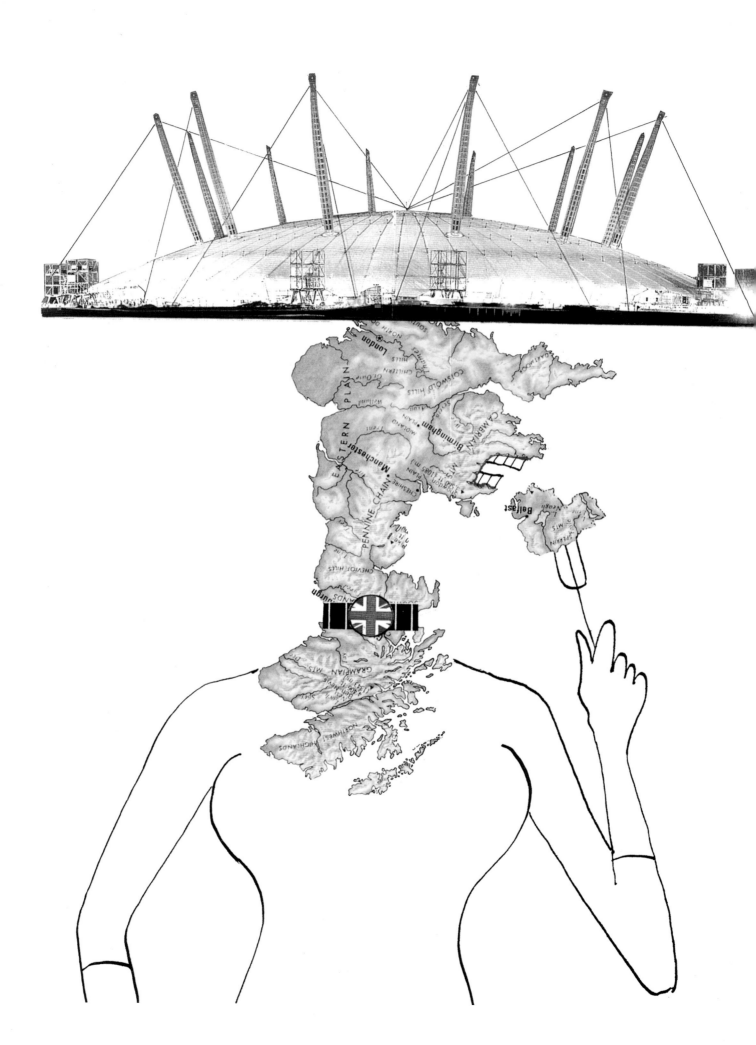

LOUIS HELLMAN

ARCHITECTURE A TO Z

A Rough Guide

To Joseph, Luke, Molly, Oliver, Ruby and the future...

First published in Great Britain in 2001 by
WILEY-ACADEMY

A division of
JOHN WILEY & SONS
Baffins Lane
Chichester
West Sussex PO19 1UD

ISBN: 0-471-48957-3

The author and publishers would like to thank those who have kindly permitted the use of images in the illustration of this book. Attempts have been made to locate all the sources of illustrations to obtain full reproduction rights, but in the very few instances where this process has failed to find the copyright holder, apologies are offered. In the case of an error, correction would be welcomed.

Other Wiley Editorial offices
New York • Wenheim • Brisbane • Singapore • Toronto

Printed and bound in Italy.

Contents

Introduction

Despite Prince Charles' "sight bite" interventions and the increasing media coverage of modern architectural matters, often of the sensational Millennium Dome "fiasco" or "wobbly bridge" variety, there is still a general ignorance about architecture, its history and relevance to our lives. While the "chattering classes" will have a smattering of knowledge about art, medicine, law or economics, you would be hard put to find anyone at a dinner party who could name, say, half a dozen architects of the 20th century.

Both in historical and contemporary terms, when architecture *is* discussed, it is invariably in purely aesthetic terms, a chronological catalogue of visual styles starting with Ancient Egypt and ending with Modern, with little analysis of the political and social forces that shape buildings. And it is even more so with contemporary architecture. The recent debate about commercial tall office towers in London has concentrated almost exclusively on shape and height, while ignoring the impact of the multinational economic powers that they serve and celebrate.

Educationally, architecture has been a "non-subject", like art but more so. Even fine art has its GCSEs, however undervalued. Yet in the Information Age children's visual and spatial awareness is increasingly sophisticated, and visual/spatial experience is the very essence of architecture.

Paradoxically, architecture has more impact on people's lives than many of the other arts. Most people live in houses or flats, go to a place of work or education, shop and visit places of entertainment, travel or health care. Each of these building types has been conceived according to some architectural principle, however basic, by those who commissioned and designed it. To understand the result we need to understand the process.

This short book is an attempt to redress the balance, to show that architecture is as much about broad *ideas* and *influences* as mere appearances. Architecture relates to, and draws upon, every field of human knowledge and experience from philosophy to plumbing, law to lighting, technology to table layouts. Today, new socio/political concerns about ecology, gender, ethnicity or Information Technology are equally impacting on architecture and changing it.

The book's alphabet format helps to avoid the art history chronological straightjacket and imposes its own conceptual order. Each essay is illustrated with cartoons and collages which reinforce the message and contrast with the straight-forward style of the text.

An index gives full details of the buildings illustrated and their architects.

Louis Hellman

 **is for architecture**

What is architecture? Here are three famous definitions...

"Frozen music"

"Commodity, firmness and delight"

"The mother of the arts"

In fact there are hundreds of definitions, which is very confusing.

What does the dictionary say? **Architecture.** *The art and science of designing and building structures.*

So architecture combines **art** and **science** (or technology) to order the environment according to people's needs.

Architecture is a form of art but not an isolated, museum art. It is an art that affects everybody. Everybody experiences architecture, like it or not.

You do not have to look at modern paintings or listen to modern music if you do not want to, but if a new building goes up in your neighbourhood you cannot avoid seeing it.

Well, it's not just a case of "seeing" it... Architecture communicates via a whole range of stimuli...

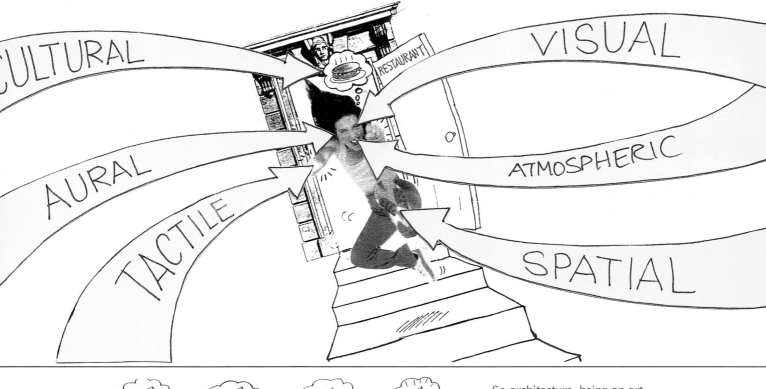

So architecture, being an art, communicates, and like all art it can be disturbing, inspiring, good, bad or sublime, depending on the aims of those who instigate it and those who design it.

Architecture is subject to wide social, political and cultural influences. It reflects the society that built it and communicates the values of that society. It is also subject to interpretation of its "meaning", which may vary depending on personal viewpoints or over time.

As an expression of social values, architecture is living history, an unwritten record as revealing as any document, and its form is subject to many influences – climatic, cultural, technological as well as social and human need. Such influences can be traced back to the beginnings of architecture, from the **Stone Age** on.

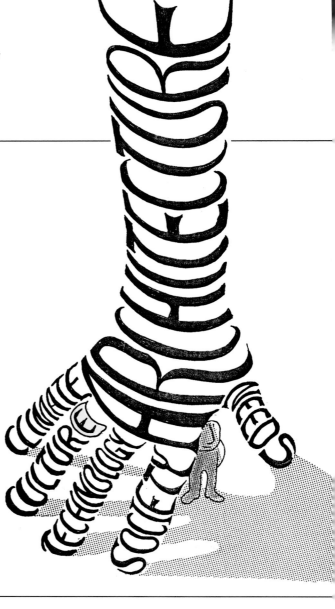

When the Great Architect in the Sky designed people She provided them with a large brain divided into two parts, one dealing with logic and reason, the other with intuition and imagination.

With this equipment people developed a tool for communication... language. Language stimulates thought and ideas, and the pooling of experience. Not just about the "real world", but also concerning spiritual matters: magic, god, life after death.

People created a spiritual environment based on ideology, with rituals relating to religion, magic or tribal loyalty.

Rituals employed signs and symbols invested with special meaning... dance, music, masks, body decoration.

For example, it may be that cave dwellers painted animals on the wall not just for aesthetic reasons but with a magical purpose, believing that if they drew an image of a fine beast before the hunt they would be more sure of killing one.

Specialist buildings evolved where the tribe's ceremonies and rituals were performed.

In contrast to dwellings, religious monuments were often large and built to last out of permanent materials.

Some still remain today. **Monoliths** or massive upright stones, called **menhirs** in France (right), were believed to contain the spirit of a god and have been made famous by Asterix the Gaul's friend Obelix. **Dolmens** (left), or huge flat stones supported on monoliths, marked tribal communal graves.

Burial places were marked, perhaps first by a simple reed shrine...

The burial place became a mound, the shrine a wooden sacrificial temple...

Eventually the mound and temple evolved into the stone-built temple.

Ever since, large buildings may be raised up on high plinths to express status.

Stonehenge in England is one of the largest Stone Age monuments. Formed of three rings of monolithic stones and continuous lintels it may have been a place for sacrificial rites, a clock or a calendar. It is not known exactly how such a complex and sophisticated structure was erected, but there are plenty of theories.

TYPICAL ARCHITECTS! ONCE THEY'VE GOT THEIR FEES YOU NEVER SEE 'EM AGAIN!

Architectural monuments evolved as an expression of primitive religious and cultural ideologies, but when society divided into elites and masses these monuments became instruments of political power.

With the discovery of metals, the Stone Age village life of tribal cooperation began to disintegrate. Metals revolutionised technology and changed society fundamentally. Tools and weapons were now more efficient. They could be moulded to any shape, resharpened or repaired.

The change from rough ore to hard metal seemed like magic and those who knew the secret of metallurgy were looked upon as magicians.

The tribe now had to produce a surplus to support the specialist metal worker who no longer needed to farm for a livelihood.

Metallurgists became itinerant, selling their skills to the highest bidder and forming a separate clan or specialist and superior class.

Instead of sharing, people accumulated personal property and possessions.

Private acquisition and wealth led to jealousy and tribal wars.

The conquering tribe made the defeated into their slaves.

Tribes were led by war chiefs who took the spoils of battle for themselves.

With the rise of class, property, wealth and power, what is known as "civilisation", came **Monumental Architecture**.

The specialist class took over religious rites, looked after the affairs of the gods and administered the surplus produce.

The priests ruled through a secondary "middle class" of specialist craftsmen and administrators.

This evolved into a secret society and soon the distinction between priest, god and king became blurred.

The priest-gods inhabited a temple built high on an artificial hill, usually by slave labour, from where they and the middle class administered the god's affairs and stored the surplus.

The temple was the largest building, raised up above the mass of ordinary dwellings and hovels, an expression of the power of the ruling elite.

Remains of these **Bronze Age** monuments can be seen in the Middle East (the **ziggurat** or holy mountain with a temple on top), in walled cities like **Ur** or **Babylon**...

in **Egypt** where the **Pharaoh's** wealth and power were channelled into the building of pyramid tombs to preserve himself and the royal family after death...

and in **Mexico** where the pre-Columbian civilisations like the **Mayans** or the **Aztecs** built vast funerary pyramids and temples dedicated to the moon or the sun.

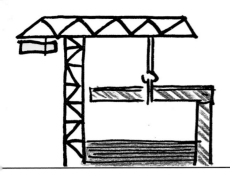 **is for building**

What's the difference between architecture and building?
Difficult one... All buildings have an architect, which means literally "chief builder", whether a professional, peasant or "do-it-yourselfer", who conceives the form of the structure.

We could say that architecture is the *concept* or *idea* which uses...

the medium of building, the *process* or *technique,* as a palette...

to communicate the reality of the original notion.

Building started from necessity. When the Great Architect designed people she made them similar to animals.

Animals are equipped with fur or claws to help them survive in their environments.

They build nests or live in natural habitats. Some even carry a shelter around with them.

People also once had hairy bodies and sharp teeth, but as they lost these they were less able to survive alone in extreme environments...

where it is very cold...   or very hot...   or very dangerous.

Young birds and animals need shelter (nests, dens or holes in the ground) but very quickly grow up and leave.

They know how to cope with the world by instinct. Bees, for example, are programmed to fly at birth.

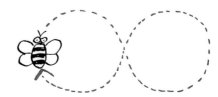

For human children the process takes much longer.

Humans are born with a few basic desires, but...

most behaviour has to be learned from the family...

or the group of families or tribe.

Human children have to be protected for more than ten years...

so the family needs to stay together for a long time...

ideally for life.

In the **Stone Age**, when people gathered and hunted food over great areas, like animals they used natural shelters, particularly **caves**, which could be protected and defended.

The Great Architect designed into people two important elements which gave them a head start over animals: a large brain and a pair of manipulative hands.

In combination these compensated for people's other deficiencies by enabling them to develop **technology**.

People made tools from natural elements in their immediate environment – sticks, stone, flints and bone – as well as...

clothes for survival in the extreme cold...

or heat...

and weapons for defence and hunting.

With tools people could also make simple shelters where no natural ones existed.

In the **New Stone Age**, it was discovered that by planting seeds, food could be grown near the home. It was not necessary to go out looking for it.

By means of agriculture, people could become food producers. Cows and sheep could be tamed and kept as walking larders and wardrobes.

Women also developed pottery, spinning, baking and brewing. Each family and social group became self-sufficient, producing all its needs.

Now people needed to live where there was good land for farming. Tools and technology enabled them to build permanent dwellings which at first resembled the old cave dwellings.

Other building forms reflected what was available in the immediate environment. Dwellings were built of...

stone in hilly places...   timber in forest areas...   skins on grassy plains...   and even ice in the Arctic.

Modern building technology is no longer dependent on local materials and character but can be much the same all over the world. Steel, glass and concrete are multinational industrialised materials, obtained from whatever global sources are cheapest or quickest.

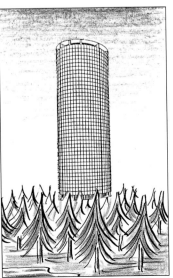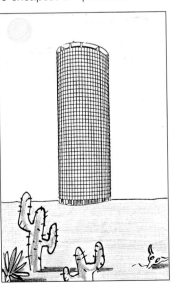

C is for climate

How shelter deals with the elements
Just to make things more interesting, the Great Architect designed in a whole lot of exciting weather around the Earth.

People's dwellings had to serve as filters to modify the external climate...

letting light, air and sun *in...*

keeping rain and noise *out...*

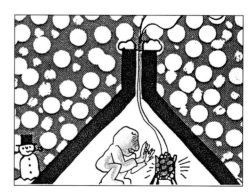

keeping the cold *out* but keeping the heat *in.*

In other words people created comfortable artificial environments within the potentially hostile natural one, using only the fabric of the building.

There are three basic types of climate in the world: hot and dry, cold and wet, or hot and humid. Dwellings have been modified to cope with these using local materials and simple environmental-control technology.

In **hot dry** areas thick walls keep out the heat by day, light colours reflect the sun's rays and small windows minimise glare. Houses close together provide shade.

At night the heat retained in the thick walls is given off to compensate for the cooler temperature. Flat roofs can be used for sleeping on when nights are hot.

Where it is **cold and wet** thick dark walls of brick or wood both keep out the cold *and* store heat from fireplaces. As the sky is less bright, larger windows are needed.

Steeply pitched roofs throw off rain and snow, while shutters protect openings from wind and cold as well as providing insulation and reducing condensation on glass.

In tropical regions where it is **hot and humid**, walls become open screens to let air pass through. Verandahs and roof overhangs provide shaded outdoor "rooms".

In the rainy season shallow sloping, overhanging roofs throw off the rain. Buildings may be up on stilts to protect against floods and keep out insects and reptiles.

Like people, buildings thrive on air to breathe. For internal comfort, air outside has to be modified against the external climate and kept moving to avoid stagnation.

Air may be tempered to deal with heat, cold, moisture and/or pollution.

Traditionally, buildings used simple means to deal with air internally, heating it with fires, cooling it with fans. But stone or brick walls were not ideal for keeping out cold, heat or damp, and in winter, windows and doors allowed heat to escape. On the other hand, chimneys and badly fitting windows helped to get rid of moisture in the air, as well as creating draughts.

Modern buildings have double outside walls to keep out heat in summer and cold in winter, double-glazed windows to keep central heating in and membranes against rising damp. But the sealed-up nature of the building means there is nowhere for the moisture in heated air to escape and this leads to condensation on colder surfaces like windows or ceilings under roofs.

The answer to problems like condensation is **air conditioning**. Air is drawn in from outside and heated, cooled, filtered and cleaned, and distributed around the building in ducts. Foul air is expelled in the same way.

Modern air-conditioned buildings with large areas of glass tend to be similar whether they are in hot or cold climates. But the sealed-up environment, where windows cannot be opened, often promote illness as well as using a great deal of electrical energy. *(See E is for ecology).*

Modern buildings also encounter other problems related to climate. Traditional "natural" materials like brick, stone or wood "weather" (mellow over time) or have decorated surfaces which conceal stains and cracks.

Modern buildings built out of steel and glass often tend to rust and deteriorate without constant and expensive maintenance.

FOR SALE
SECOND HAND
BUILDING
BODYWORK NEEDS
SOME ATTENTION

Traditional, low buildings were often grouped to provide a protective "microclimate". But when buildings went tall they disrupted the natural climate, creating wind turbulance at ground level or casting large shadows over neighbouring communities.

is for design

The Great Architect designed the world in six days, but buildings usually take a bit longer.

Design and planning, or the setting up of a strategy prior to action, is the most important part of any operation, whether it be a military battle or headed notepaper.

It is essential for buildings, which require large financial and organisational resources and usually need to last for generations.

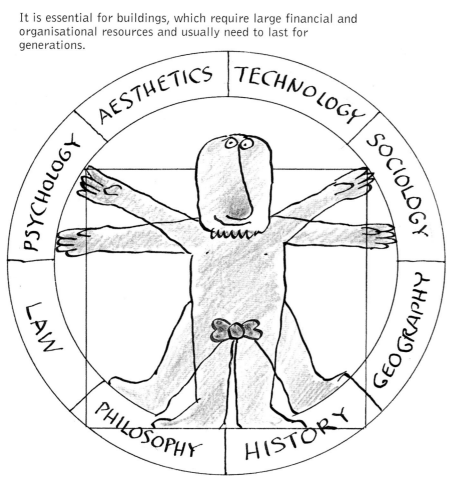

Working out and coordinating the myriad ingredients that comprise modern buildings is an exacting task that requires a wide range of skills. Architectural design is not just a matter of styling or producing seductive drawings. From conception to completion, it is a complex process which involves practically all aspects of human activity from philosophy to plumbing, law to lighting, technology to table layouts.

Historically, monumental architecture followed established building forms evolved through tradition and the requirements of religious rites or secular power.

Pyramids and temples in Ancient Egypt changed relatively little in over 4000 years.

Greek temples, derived from timber hut shrines, were like large sculptures and were often designed by sculptor/architects.

Roman architecture was a product of military engineering and Greek models, but on a vast scale.

Medieval cathedrals evolved by trial and error, and combined Roman plans and local building forms.

Renaissance architecture recreated Greek and Roman classical building using medieval technology.

By the **19th century**, industrialised technology gave rise to specialised professions in addition to architects.

Architects now headed a design team comprising structural engineers, quantity surveyors, electrical and mechanical engineers, landscape architects and interior designers, each of whom dealt with various specialised aspects of building.

But the architect is the only building industry professional who is trained as a generalist designer and has a view or vision of the whole building and its relation to the environment in which it is placed.

The raw materials of building design are the requirements of the client who commissions the building, and the building's users (the brief), and the characteristics of the land (the site) and its surroundings. The brief is vital; it is said that no building can be better than its brief.

Design is in two stages, including some of the following:

PRELIMINARY DESIGN

Surveying the site for orientation, wind direction, trees, access, view, etc.

Preparing draft designs for discussion with the client and approval.

Final design drawings for making a planning application to the local authority.

DETAILED DESIGN

Preparing detailed technical drawings with the engineering consultants.

Satisfying the requirements of building, fire, health, safety and access regulations

Drawing up detailed specifications covering materials and workmanship.

Further design modifications may have to be made during the building contract. Even the most carefully worked out design on paper cannot predict every eventuality in practice.

The basic means of communicating architectural design is through scale drawings depicting **plans**, **sections** and **elevations**. Once this "language" is understood, the form of the proposed building can be "read" on paper by cross-referencing the three representations. For lay people, unfamiliar with the language, architects may also use other devices such as perspective drawings, models or computer simulations.

THE PLAN

 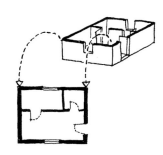

Plans are the equivalent of slicing horizontally through a building at each floor to show as many features as possible: walls, windows, doors, openings. A "**north point**" shows the building's orientation.

THE SECTION

Sections are the equivalent of slicing vertically through a building to show as many features as possible; they may be taken widthways or lengthways. As in plans, walls are shown in heavy line.

THE ELEVATION

 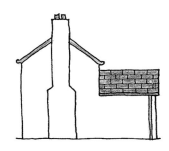

North (front) elevation   **West (side) elevation**

Elevations are drawings of each face of the building and are normally labelled according to their orientation; "south elevation" indicates that the elevation faces south.

SCALE

1 to 50   **1 to 100**

Drawings to accurate scale miniaturise the size of the building. For example, a scale of 1 to 100 means 1 centimetre on the drawing is equivalent to 1 metre actual size in the building.

The architect may be compared to both the composer of the music and the conductor of an orchestra. Architectural plans are like musical scores and, in a similar fashion, can be interpreted on many levels by those who can read them. Like scores, they may be beautiful in themselves, but their function is to be blueprints for the performance – the building. Architecture is the concept, first in the architect's mind, then on paper and finally realised through the instruments – the building materials. The architect coordinates the tempo and melody produced by all the players involved.

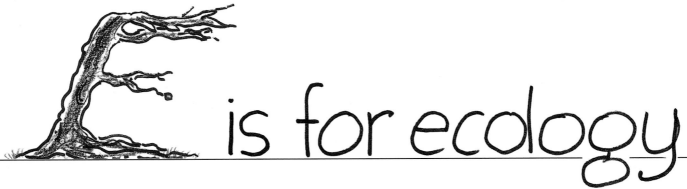

E is for ecology

The youth culture of the 1960s challenged the dominance of both Western industrial capitalism and state socialism, which were seen as socially and environmentally destructive in the same measure as the benefits they brought. For both, the architectural expression had become that of the **Modern Movement**, collective, anonymous and over-reliant on technology. The "alternative society", like the 19th-century romantics, looked to a previous era when people cooperated, lived in harmony with nature and were self-sufficient. Alternative architecture, made from recycled industrial products, reliant on low technology and serviced by energy from solar or wind power, also opted out of "the system".

For a time the abundance of alternative ideas and ways of living shook the political establishment, but by the 1970s these had dissipated or were absorbed by the pop music and fashion industries. The naively idealistic dream went sour and the state took an even firmer grip.

But the 1973 oil crisis, when Middle Eastern states increased the price of oil to the West (and architects, as always, flocked to the source of new money), and the realisation that fossil fuels such as coal were finite, led governments to look at ways of saving energy. Buildings consume over 60% of all energy and modern buildings, relying on air conditioning, central heating and artificial ventilation, represent a substantial proportion of this.

Governments were unwilling to curb the industrial producers in any radical sense, and the energy-saving measures they imposed tended to be minimal: additional insulation or double glazing, for example. But research into alternative "free" sources of immense power from the sun, wind, earth or water had been undertaken since the 1920s and was gradually adopted in experimental self-sufficient dwellings.

By the 1980s the effects of untramelled large-scale industrial production became apparent through global warming, holes in the Earth's ozone layer and the pollution of air and land. Solutions to this reflected different directions in scientific development.

On the one hand, **biology** discovered ever more interventionist means of controlling nature through biotechnology and genetic engineering. This reinforced the notion of "spaceship Earth". High technology would solve the problems it had created; the Earth still represented a stockpile of resources to be exploited and modified.

On the other hand, the **physical sciences** had rejected the old Newtonian model of the universe as conforming to a fixed pattern of inert atoms in favour of a holistic view of the cosmos as fluid, indeterminate, spontaneous and chaotic. Humankind, far from being apart from and in control of this process, was inseparable from it.

Two alternative approaches to the notion of a "green" architecture
follow from current developments in science.

One is the high-tech building-as-machine, or "intelligent building", employing up-to-date information technology with all aspects of the building fabric controlled, monitored or modified by a central "brain".

A central computer controls heating, cooling, cooking, washing, security, information, decoration and entertainment.

A cellular external "skin" responds to the external climate and modifies the internal environment accordingly.

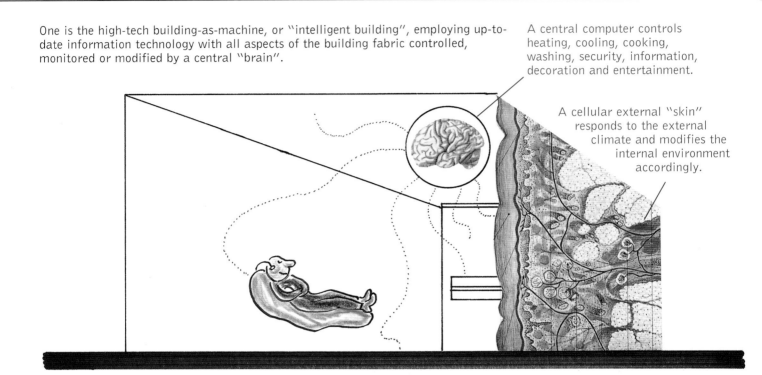

The other may be termed the "passive" approach where the building is as self-sufficient as possible, not relying on any "artificial" supplies of power or services, and is sited to exploit natural "free" sources of energy.

Wind pump on high ground

Natural ventilation stacks prevent condensation

Solar panels provide electricity

Conservatory acts as heat store in winter

Barrier on north side and protection from wind

Rainwater collector and waste recycler

Thick insulation to retain heat in winter and keep it out in summer

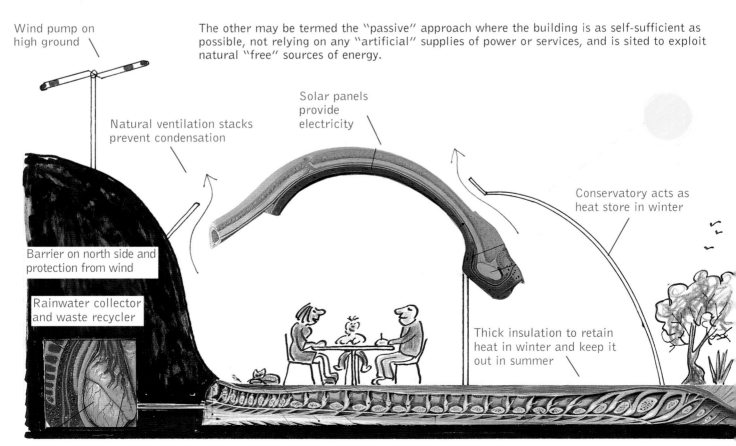

In practice, current architecture usually combines aspects of both ideals.

Not only do buildings need large amounts of energy to service them, but the production of the components they are built of — steel, glass, aluminium, plastic or wood — equally consumes natural resources as well as adding to pollution.

Transporting materials...   manufacture...   transporting components...   construction

The current goal of "sustainability" implies building to last with materials which are from renewable sources or employ minimum energy in production, and have low maintenance. For example, timber is a good organic, renewable source — it grows on trees — and has good structural, insulating and aesthetic properties.
But not all timber is suitable. Rainforests are still being plundered for tropical hardwoods such as mahogany, which may have taken 400 years to grow. This destroys the ecological balance, wildlife, soil and sources of medicines. An area the size of England and Wales is denuded in Amazon-basin forests each year. Younger, and thus renewable, sources of hardwoods and softwoods are readily available from North America.

Since the 1960s, recycling old building materials has been another means of reducing energy consumption. Hippy communes built shelters from discarded cars, food cans, plastic containers and other detritus of the consumer society.

Today there are agencies for salvaging bricks, tiles, windows, doors and other reusable components from demolished buildings.

F is for futurism

Futurism was launched by an avant-garde group of Italian artists and architects in 1909 with Marinetti's *Futurist Manifesto,* but it might be extended to include the various visions of a brave new world conjured up by modern architects after the First World War.

Images of futuristic cities have been an obsession in architecture since then.

After the war it seemed as if the old order of empires and nation states had been swept away for good and a new world "fit for heroes" would be created.

Pioneer modern architects saw themselves as leaders in the creation of the new utopia, starting from a clean sheet. Tradition and history would be ignored as irrelevant. The New Order would be determined by science, technology and especially machines – the exciting new aeroplanes, ships, trains and motor cars developed at the end of the previous century.

The traditional language of architecture would be eradicated along with the bourgeois *fin-de-siècle* hierarchical society it served, and be replaced by machine-made forms. The designers of buildings would no longer be individual artists but anonymous groups of engineer/technicians.

The vision of an architectural utopia was fuelled by the revolutionary ideas of the four great "architects" of the 20th century: Einstein, Marx, Freud and Darwin.

Albert Einstein (1897–1955) in his Theory of Relativity demonstrated that the world and the universe were not arranged according to some grand fixed master plan but were continually changing. Change was the only certain element. To the three dimensions of length, height and breadth was added a fourth: time.

This consciousness of space and time found expression in the forms of the new architecture which seemed to extend out to infinity, the outside walls dissolved into glass. Buildings were given a three-dimensional quality which seemed best appreciated from a speeding car or plane.

FUTURISM

Italy, recently unified and just beginning to industrialise, was not inhibited by an industrial heritage and was able to adopt the latest technological advances. The Futurist artists and architects did not merely accept the machine, they worshipped it, and rejected all past forms. The racing car was seen to be more beautiful than a Greek statue.

Art and architecture would exhibit all the dynamic streamlined qualities of the fast new machines of transport.

A vision of how whole cities would be transformed by the new machine-made world had been projected in a series of drawings by the Italian Futurist architect **Sant 'Elia** in 1914. The multilevel buildings of the New City were influenced by American skyscrapers as well as power stations and bridges. Moving elements like lifts were placed on the outside.

Karl Marx (1818–83) saw history following an inevitable pattern of class conflict and worker exploitation that would lead to the overthrow of capitalism and the emergence of a new classless, collectivist and collaborative socialist society of unalienated human beings where the state would ultimately wither away.

His theories fed the Bolshevist revolution in Russia in 1917 and led to the overthrow of the old Tsarist regime.

CONSTRUCTIVISM

Like Italy, Russia had started to industrialise late and in the heady anarchic days after the revolution young architects, inspired by the Futurists, German modernism and Cubist and abstract art, drew buildings that expressed a synthesis of progressive urban architectural ideas and the new social order.

The style was termed Constructivism under the slogan "Down with Art! Long live technology!" Dynamic building forms, stripped down to the bare frames of their structure and exposing lifts and stairs, incorporated searchlights, neon signs, graphics, aerials, and cine equipment. Factory forms and abstract art were meant to appeal to the newly liberated proletariat.

But the movement built few buildings Russia did not have the technology required and by the 1930s Stalin had clamped down on all forms of avant-garde art, approving only the overblown, stripped-classical monumental architecture beloved of totalitarian dictators everywhere.

Sigmund Freud (1856–1939) was the architect of 20th-century psychological man, who was no longer ruled by reason applied to external phenomena but by psychological forces. The 19th-century Romantic movement had believed intuitively in much the same process but now it was thought that these forces could be measured or predicted scientifically by analysis. Analysis employed metaphor and symbolism to attempt to understand the workings of the subconscious.

EXPRESSIONISM

In postwar Germany, now polarised between the forces of the left and right, the Expressionist style adopted by artists, architects, film makers and novelists could be seen as the application of anti-rationalist psychological ideas to the arts. The movement was, however, as short-lived as the democratic Weimar Republic.

In architecture, free-flowing or jagged forms inspired by natural forms sought to express, not just speed and mechanisation as the Futurists had done, but industrial power, energy or even political progress as well as conscious or sub-conscious sexual symbolism.

Charles Darwin (1809–82) had shown that animal behaviour was highly adapted to, and conditioned by, the environment. So could not the equation be reversed? Provide the "correct" environment and "correct" behaviour would necessarily evolve. And if this could be achieved for animals, why not for human beings in society?

FUNCTIONALISM

Pioneer modern architects between the two world wars preached a form of Darwinian theory known as Functionalism, a supposedly rational and "scientific" approach to design. Its catch phrase was "**form follows function**", meaning that the form of a building would be determined by the function it was to fulfil, not some artistic preconception. It followed that these "rational" buildings and cities would in turn determine a new breed of inhabitant in a new society. Architects would become social engineers rather than artists.

We shape our buildings and our buildings shape us.   Winston Churchill

The great Swiss architect **Le Corbusier** (qv) drew images of such rational and functional cities separated into zones for work, living, transport and leisure, which influenced town planning for decades to come. Le Corbusier hated the "irrational mess" of old cities like Paris and proposed rebuilding it along rational lines on a rigid grid of motorways with serried ranks of office towers housing the business industrialist controllers of society. A self-fulfilling prophecy!

is for gothic

The more powerful a society's rulers become, the more splendid, vast and awe-inspiring is the monumental architecture that expresses this power, whether tombs, temples, palaces or churches. As the Roman Catholic Church gained control of Europe in the **Middle Ages**, its power was exercised through a new architecture which exalted its triumph: the Gothic.

The Pope in Rome was now like an emperor, more powerful than any king or prince. The **Holy Roman Empire** had taken over the Imperial Roman network, and its buildings.

The French monarchy had become rich and influential and was the Pope's main ally. Gothic developed in a small area around Paris – the **Ile de France,** which was the Capetian kings' main domain – during the 11th and 12th centuries. As the kings' power grew they needed an educated administration, and since education was monopolised by the Church, bishops became powerful at court. They built large new churches-cum-1 palaces, Gothic cathedrals, on sites donated by the king, who also sold land to influential townsmen in return for support in the face of threats from the aristocracy.

Gothic symbolised a new synthesis of humanity, God and nature. Previously God had been thought of as an unknown and terrible force. Romanesque (*see R is for Rome*) churches reflected this in their darkness and mystery. Decoration was often grotesque and surreal, depicting strange serpents or devils. Representations of saints and people showed them with identical and anonymous features.

But now Church scholars in the new cathedral-based universities believed that God revealed Himself in His creations, in people and nature. The Church building became an image of nature, imitating plant forms with ribs, stems or fronds, and seeming to grow out of the earth like lines of trees with interlocking foliage. Statues were recognisable portraits of individuals.

The Gothic system of construction exploited three elements: the POINTED ARCH (A), the FLYING BUTTRESS (B) and the RIBBED VAULT (C).

Once chisels superseded hammers, stone technology was continually refined and developed by trial and error into an architecture of tension, rhythm and equilibrium, where columns and tracery became as slender as plants and as delicate as lace.

In the Gothic church, the heavy walls of the old Romanesque style disappear. The roof and **vault** are now carried via bridge-like supports (the **flying buttresses**) to huge free-standing supporting walls at right angles outside, allowing large window openings in the outside walls proper (D). This neatly mirrors the medieval social structure of the monarch supported by the clergy and buttressed by the merchant class.

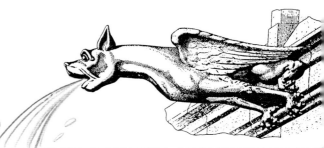

IT'S THE SPITTING IMAGE!

The whole of the Gothic cathedral was a teaching and propaganda tool: an image of heaven on earth, a heavenly city, both inside and out.

The west entrance front depicted the gate into heaven, often incorporating sculptures of the Last Judgement, Christ and the Apostles, the good souls and the damned. The sides were equally covered in sculptures representing the temporal world, often with portraits of local dignitaries or the stone masons themselves. Like classical temples, the exterior and interior were painted in multi-colours.

The Gothic style was adapted to local climates and conditions. In the north, rainwater was thrown off steep roofs by **gargoyles**, spouts carved into grotesque beasts.

Cathedrals had patrons, architects and building contractors, but these tended to be from the same elite group – the monks or the clergy – with similar aims and ideals. Money was raised through the sale of relics and indulgences to the common people, who might also work as labourers on the churches.

Internally, the strong vertical lines of the structure divided up the space in mathematical proportions like a musical rhythm, representing God's ordering of humanity and nature. Above was the Vault of Heaven, lit from small windows high up.

Because of the slender nature of the outside wall columns, large windows were possible. They were filled with didactic stained-glass pictures to teach religion to the mainly illiterate congregation – pictures of light.

Light had a special meaning: the oneness of God, light (enlightenment) and beauty.

12th century media...

20th century media...

With the expansion of towns in the **Middle Ages**, a new society evolved alongside that of the feudal countryside. International maritime trade flourished once more and towns sited on river estuaries, like Venice, Genoa and Pisa in Italy and Antwerp in the north, grew rapidly. Royal charters encouraged merchants, aldermen and landowners to set up local governments and these rapidly became a challenge to established authority.

Again, this was expressed in architecture. The new merchant princes used their wealth and power to erect large urban secular buildings in the Gothic style (previously exclusive to castles or churches): town halls, guild halls, market halls or colleges.

Venice grew rich on trade with the East. In the 14th century the city's princely ruler, the Doge, built a palace in a flamboyantly and Eastern-influenced Gothic style.

In the north, **Flanders** was well-positioned to take advantage of both sea routes and farming. Here the cloth trade quickly expanded, using wool bought from England.

Craftworkers and merchants had formed **guilds** to fix prices and control who was allowed to practise these trades. Members of the stonemasons' guild were not tied to any one town or country but hawked their expertise internationally. Their guild guarded their secrets, the most vital being the ability to construct large buildings from small drawings. There was no standard measure.

Dimensions had to be transferred from drawing to building by using a method of proportion...

scaling off the drawing with a compass and multiplying it on the building material where it was cut with chisels.

Master masons were sculptors as well as builders, and were often the architects of the cathedral or church.

The Gothic style ruled until the Renaissance
and the revival of classical architecture.

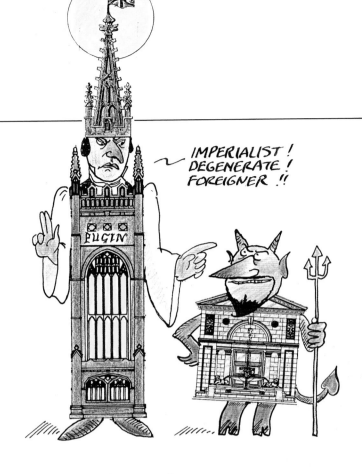

But with the rise of Romanticism and Nationalism in 19th-century England and Germany there was a renewed interest in medieval art and architecture. Classicism was seen to be an expression of the old imperial regimes, an imported, "foreign" and imposed style.

In England **Pugin** (1812–1852) saw Gothic not merely as a style, but the one true, honest, natural, democratic, free *English* architecture (although it had, of course, originated in France) and led the way to the **Gothic Revival**, an embodiment of moral and political values.

The economic expansion of Great Britain and its empire in the 19th century inspired a reaction to the dominance of classical art and architecture and a desire to promote a national, Nordic culture. (See also *V is for Vernacular*.)

In England the aristocracy was more flexible than other regimes in the exercise of power and absorbed the emerging middle-class industrialists, and their wealth, into existing institutions, as well as giving them (male property owners) the vote in 1832. When the new **Houses of Parliament** were built three years later they combined a formal Neo-Classical plan by one architect (Charles Barry) with Gothic Revival facades by another (Pugin), neatly symbolising the marriage of the old establishment with the new money.

" WELCOME TO THE CLUB, OLD BOY ! "

is for housing

The concept of "housing" and the "housing problem" is allied to the rapid growth of urban populations since the 18th century. "Housing" is defined to include not merely dwellings, but the supporting context, services and infrastructure associated with domestic living.

A consequence of 18th-century industrialisation was that rural workers flocked to towns and cities to work in factories, around which the owners built cramped back-to-back housing without running water, sanitation or artificial light. Polluted by fumes and noise, the dark, airless streets were breeding grounds for poverty, disease and, eventually, socialism in the meagre corner pubs.

At the same time the new middle classes moved away from the effects and sources of their wealth to new developments in the inner and outer suburbs. These consisted of terraced housing grouped round leafy squares and crescents, and provided with gardens, servants' quarters, coach houses, private roads and security and, later, plumbing, sanitation, sewers and gas lighting as well as an infrastructure of shops and churches.

The reaction to the deprivations of the industrial city and, following biological science's demonstration that clean, sunny environments lessened disease, a desire for air, sun, clean water and green space for all resulted in the idea of the garden city. This evolved from the 19th-century **Arts and Crafts Movement**'s critique of the industrial society and a new Romanticism which sought to reconcile man and nature, work and pleasure. **Garden cities** were idealised communities modelled on an expanded version of the traditional village or suburb but with individual houses and gardens, parks, shops, pubs, and allotments, served by railways and adjacent to the countryside. *Rus in urbe.*

Between the two world wars, the problem of urban land shortages and the growth of cities was addressed by the Modern Movement, which combined the garden city ideals of open green, airy spaces with advanced building technology and Cubist-inspired blocks of flats provided with electricity, central heating, modern bathrooms and labour-saving kitchens. Now the attempted reconciliation was between *mechanisation* and nature.

In **Germany**, local authorities in the shaky **Weimar Republic** built housing for the organised work force according to the new model: white, pure, healthy. Rejecting the garden city layouts of houses and streets, the developments comprised long, low blocks with landscaped spaces in between. Many blocks were prefabricated. Whole walls were manufactured in factories and assembled on site to minimise labour costs. Unfortunately, this put thousands of building workers out of work and contributed to the growing unemployment.

After the **Second World War**, politicians were generally persuaded that the **Modern Movement's** housing solutions – large prefabricated blocks of apartments set in parkland – were the answer to slum clearance and the development of empty bombed sites. People would be taught new ways of living.

Building high would be economic in land use *and* construction costs. Traditional methods of building in brick or timber were far too slow for the task in hand. Prefabricated walls made in factories and rapidly hoisted into position by tower cranes was the 20th-century answer. Central heating, modern bathrooms and kitchens of a high standard would be provided by modern technology. Ex-slum dwellers' lives would be transformed by the new clean, light and airy environments. That was the hypothesis to be applied on a vast scale without any previous experimental testing.

But politicians wanted solutions on the cheap. They were not willing to provide the resources that would compensate for the loss of amenities people enjoyed when living at ground level, or the associated social infrastructure. All over the world traditional communities were broken up and displaced into high-rise, state-owned workers' blocks. Families with children were isolated, the old inter-dependence and self-help destroyed. There were no shops, pubs or parks, just "units of accommodation" and cheap lifts that constantly broke down. By the 1970s the estates became dumping grounds for "problem families"

While workers were ghettoised into inner city, high-rise, watered-down versions of pioneer Modern Movement housing, the middle class moved to the outer suburbs in equally diluted models of the garden city developed by speculative builders. Modernists had condemned the suburbs for their wasteful sprawl, lack of planning and alienated bourgeois life styles. Yet in England eight million people had been rehoused in this way during 20 years of interwar depression. In the USA and Europe suburbs developed as a result of improved systems of transport communication to the city and increased lower-middle-class prosperity. Despite the scorn of architects, who probably live in converted old buildings in the inner city, suburbia is popular, although the demands of car-ownership, run-down public transport systems, plastic double-glazing and out-of-town hypermarkets have somewhat tarnished the utopian ideal.

THEN...   ...AND NOW

A drastic solution to the worst failures of "high-rise" housing ghettos from the 1970s on was demolition and replacement with more suitable "low-rise" family homes. But this represented an enormous waste of resources over time.

A less wasteful approach was to provide the management and maintenance which had been lacking when housing was built in the 1960s for a less violent society where crime, drugs, vandalism and single-parent families were not so rife.

A third "solution" was privatisation. Public sector housing, often in prime inner city locations, could be sold off on the open market to relatively affluent buyers to be upgraded.

In other words, it was not the architecture that was at fault but the system of dispensing ideologically-driven housing solutions to people who lacked resources, choice or control.

The alternative to authoritarian public sector housing schemes, in terms of giving tenants some control over their design and location, has been proposed by some architects since the late 1960s but in practice has rarely been achieved. The ideal solution is for people to build their own homes with state subsidies but this is naturally restricted by their own capability and urban land availability.

The builders of private sector volume housing continue to offer suburban houses, which are often poorly designed and planned and wasteful of land, in mock-traditional styles but using modern materials such as plastic. Architects yearn to be involved in this industry and provide well-designed, modern, energy-saving, high-density, high-quality housing. But the powerful interests of speculative builders and their advertising clout ensure that mediocrity rules.

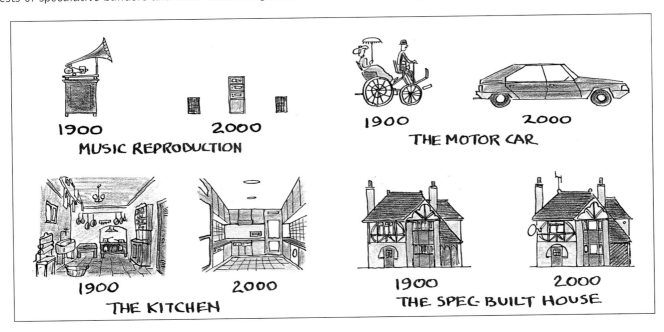

1900   2000
MUSIC REPRODUCTION

1900   2000
THE MOTOR CAR

1900   2000
THE KITCHEN

1900   2000
THE SPEC-BUILT HOUSE

I is for industrial

The main impetus to the development of capitalism in England in the late 18th century was the **Industrial Revolution**, the change from handcraft to machine mass production and the subsequent migration of workers from the countryside to the towns and cities.

This revolution evolved from the **Age of Reason** and the quest for knowledge about the physical world. Inventors, entrepreneurs and industrialists competed in a *laissez-faire* economy devoid of controls, making fortunes from factory production using cheap labour and raw materials culled from the **British Empire**. New wealth demanded new building types: factories, mills, dockland warehouses and so on.

"I'LL JUST HAVE A WORD WITH MY SUPPLIER!"

But architects did not consider the new industrial buildings to be architecture, or that the ravages caused by the Industrial Revolution were their concern. However, they served the new capitalists by dressing up their mansions in grandiose historical styles: Gothic, Renaissance, Baroque, Egyptian or Greek. They also formed professional closed shops to stop undercutting amateurs from getting their hands on the new source of loot.

Metals like iron had been used in buildings for centuries, in the form of door handles, window frames or fixings, usually beaten out by the local blacksmith. But the discovery of how to smelt iron ore using coke in a blast furnace meant that large quantities of standardised components could be cast in moulds, and mass-produced to make not only machines but also structural members. Stronger, more resistant and more durable than timber, they could be erected more quickly.

Engineers versed in the new iron technology replaced architects as creative inventors of new structures. Using mass-produced iron (and later steel) components, they designed new structures to house the machines of the new industrialists of a scale and lightness never dreamed of before.

Techniques for building by hand, slow and labour-intensive, and employing a limited range of materials (brick, stone, wood, etc), had evolved through a mutative process over a long period of time by...

TRIAL...

and ERROR...

until traditions of good building were established.

But in the 19th century, both materials and techniques were revolutionised in a short space of time. Parts of buildings could be made in factories and quickly assembled on site.

One of the best known of these was the **Crystal Palace** designed by **Joseph Paxton** to house the **Great Exhibition** of 1851 in London and display the products from Britain and her empire. Evolving from greenhouse designs, but on a vast scale, and taking only six months to make and erect, it was the wonder of the age (except to most architects). Internally it was a seemingly endless, barely enclosed space, a fitting symbol of the free and unlimited possibilities for British capitalism and imperialism.

By the beginning of the 20th century, **Germany** and the **USA** (qv) had overtaken Britain as the major industrial powers and were the main impetus to the development of the modern architectural style that machine production had spawned.

In Germany, newly unified under the Prussian military aristocracy (the Junkers), military-style planning, machine production and state-controlled land ownership enabled the state to develop giant new concerns in the steel, chemicals and electrical industries.

German architects studied the new British architecture which had emerged from the Arts and Crafts Movement's study of the **vernacular** (qv) and were impressed by its pure, clean forms, relatively free from decoration or ornament, and ideal for machine production.

German architects (unlike their British counterparts) now changed their view of the machine. It was gradually seen as the salvation of architecture and with its use a new **modern** (qv) architecture appropriate to the 20th century would be created. Organisations like the **Werkbund**, set up in 1907, aimed to bring together industry and designers to promote both efficient good design and the greater glory of the Fatherland. A marriage was arranged between art and the machine and the languages of architecture and industrial capitalism started to converge.

The happy couple moved into their new home, the factory – the perfect expression of the new partnership designed for the convenience of machines rather than workers. The style was known as the **Machine Aesthetic**, and factories like that built for the massive AEG electrical concern were the new temples, the new cathedrals of power.

Throughout the 20th century modern architects have been obsessed with the notion of industrialised buildings – not just mass-produced components, but whole buildings that roll off the conveyor belts as in car production, complete with prefabricated bathrooms and kitchens, and using advanced technology to achieve a high standard. Ready-made houses, for example, could be dropped onto sites by helicopters in minutes. Unfortunately, buildings are not like machines; they have far more complex cultural, functional and human ingredients. The dream may work for one building, but multiplied a million times?

" I THINK MY BIG END'S GONE ! "

At the start of a new century and a new millennium, Western society is once more in a state of transition...

With the **Agrarian Revolution** people related directly to the land.

With the Industrial Revolution people related to machines.

In a **Post-Industrial** society people will relate to **information technology**.

It is now recognised that massive industrialisation has brought as many problems as benefits, threatening the very health and **ecology** (qv) of the Earth and its population through pollution and the greedy exploitation of natural resources. The information revolution enables us to monitor and control industrial production as just one element in a menu of ingredients to improve existence. Architecture, as always, follows where society leads.

TECHNOLOGY IS THE ANSWER..! NOW WHAT'S THE QUESTION ?

is for japan

Japanese architecture, like Japanese culture and society, was influenced by **China** but modified and refined according to Japan's particular island geography and climate and the uniqueness of the Japanese character. Japan is three-quarters mountains and forests and prone to earthquakes and typhoons as well as heat (the very name **Nippon** means the origin of the sun). Japanese buildings, therefore, employed light timber frames which could "ride" the effects of earthquakes, steep roofs to throw off rain, projecting up-turned eaves as protection from the sun and were raised up on stilts in case of floods.

But as well as responding to functional requirements, Japanese architecture is an expression of a particular spiritual and religious relationship with nature. As in China, the political and social structure did not foster monumental churches or palaces, and stone walling was confined to the castles of the war lords who ruled over feudal fiefdoms until the 19th century. It was not until **Buddhism** was introduced from India via China in the 7th century that any idea of permanence or posterity intruded into the Eastern notion of time as a holistic and nonlinear entity. The philosophy of **Zen Buddhism**, with its reverence for natural simplicity, and concentration on detail, perfection and ritual, further refined design.

The original religion, **Shintoism**, treated places as sacred, each with its own god, and sometimes marked with a simple thatched-roof shrine.

Buddhist monasteries were sacred enclosures where the route (**The Way**) between temples, gateways and shrines was as important as individual buildings.

Samurai warriors also built forts and castles that had stone wall plinths and rose to five storeys usually with a central tower for look-out and defence.

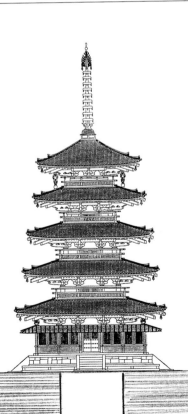

Buddhist
wooden **pagodas**,
multistoreyed shrines
attached to monasteries,
were also imported from China.
These series of roofs piled up around
a central structure are tree-like in form
(trunk and branches) and, like trees, can
resist a certain amount of earth
movement.

The traditional Japanese house, built of slim untreated wood framing (2), had sliding rice-paper-covered walls (3) to open up the interior space or the inside to the outside. The floor plan and the size of the house were determined by combinations of standard-sized modular mats (1).

There was hardly any furniture, **futons** were brought out for sleeping and the whole domestic environment was minimal, ritualised and ordered.

Tea houses, to accommodate the tea drinking ceremony, were a variation on the typical house with additional facilities.

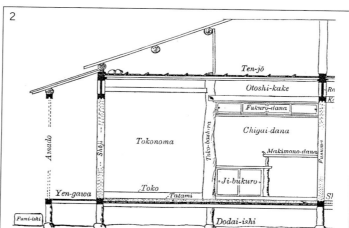

For centuries Japanese society remained unknown at the "edge of the world", despite intrusions by the Spaniards in the 16th century. But in 1854 Japan opened up to American trade and influence and Western technology. The old feudal system ended and Western-style organisation, militarism and industrialisation eventually made Japan the most powerful state in the Far East.

The beauty of newly-discovered Japanese art, particularly prints, influenced the **Impressionist** and **Post-Impressionist** painters like **Van Gogh** as well as the **Art Nouveau** movement. The simplicity, delicate framed structures, untreated materials, spatial relationship between inside and outside and modular nature of Japanese architecture had a great influence on the early 20th-century Modern Movement. The American architect **Frank Lloyd Wright** (qv) was influenced by Japanese woodcuts and took up the Japanese approach of untreated materials and the opening up of the dwelling to the outside. **Mies van der Rohe** in Germany was influenced by the minimalist and modular nature of Japanese architecture, borrowing from **Lao Tsu** the epithet "less is more" (there is a richness in simplicity and refinement) which he translated into steel and glass, modular mass production and flexible internal spaces.

THE ELIMINATION OF THE INSIGNIFICANT!

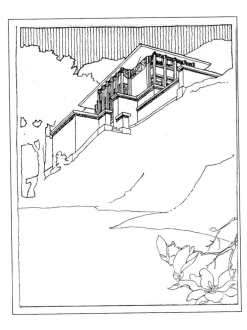

LESS IS MORE (MORE OR LESS!)

As in Germany, the destruction of Japan's industrial base along with her military dictatorship at the end of the Second World War prepared the ground for rapid economic renewal and growth, assisted by American aid, and her emergence as a world superpower. This was achieved through a handful of paternalistic industrial giants exerting control over government and workforce alike.

Power and wealth promotes monumental architecture. Not having any tradition of large-scale building, Japan had adopted Western styles since the 19th century. After the war, some attempt was made to reconcile tradition and modernity in concrete structures that evoked timber-frame detailing writ large. In post-**Hiroshima** Japan there was in addition a desire to annihilate the past and this chimed with Modern Movement objectives.

With the post-1960s "economic miracle", and consequent urban expansion, Western high-density solutions were applied indiscriminately. As the only non-Western world power Japan adopted the **International Modern, Post-Modern, High-Tech and anti-architecture Pop** styles as well as importing the West's most avant-garde ideas and architects and exporting the work of its own star architects to Europe and America. Outside cities and towns, Post-Modernist inclusiveness enabled a return to the traditions of harmonising with landscape and treating sun, light and the elements as ingredients in design.

 **is for kids**

Kids' needs are often way down on the list of priorities when it comes to the design of the environment, particularly in dense, dangerous and dirty urban situations.

Where playgrounds are provided by local authorities they are often of the traditional type with fixed equipment on hard surfaces. These are fairly popular with parents and small children but tend to exclude older children or teenagers. In other words, what the playgrounds gain on the roundabouts they lose on the swings.

Alternative sculptural play structures have been developed by architects but, like some modern architecture, they seem more for the entertainment of the designers than the users.

In the 1960s, following consultation with children, the concept of the "adventure playground" was developed as an alternative to the traditional fixed swings and roundabouts model, giving both young and older children the freedom to exercise their imagination and create their own play environment using materials provided. Unfortunately this freedom often led to abuse and vandalism and by the late 1970s many such areas were closed.

Today much of a child's play environment is provided ready-packaged by television, computer games or vast commercial theme parks which stimulate consumption through advertising as part of the market economy. As ever, grown-ups fear these will replace self-discovery and creativity but in effect they add sophisticated fuel to children's imaginations, and books and traditional construction toys are as popular as ever.

School and school playground design illustrates the way architecture can serve and reflect educational, social and political objectives.

In the late 19th century general state education was instituted and an extensive programme of specially designed schools in urban areas embarked upon. Schools were based on strict hierarchical principles. Classrooms, with high windows to prevent "distractions", contained regimented rows of desks in front of the teacher and blackboard. Externally the buildings perpetuated a severe ecclesiastical Gothic style, monumental and austere. Playgrounds were hard tarmac rectangles surrounded by chain-link fencing.

The early 20th century saw further state reforms as a distinction was made between primary and secondary education. After the **Second World War**, and the development of welfare states, a massive programme of new school building was under way, and in Britain a new school opened on average once a day from the 1950s until the 1970s.

In the 1960s progressive principles were applied to **primary** school education, encouraging **child-centred learning** by inquiry and experience in small **mixed-ability** groups. The old "chalk and talk" system was ousted. Modern architecture, light, flexible and open-planned, responded to the new philosophy if not always to the idea of the building as a robust teaching tool for people.

By the late 1970s the old modern flat-roofed glass-box image of the school gave way to richer forms with the scale of the primary school related to the children: low window sills, small tables and chairs, mini-toilets and so on.

Covered glazed areas linked the building to the outside which was landscaped to provide informal hard or soft areas for teaching or play.

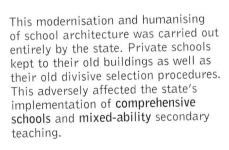

WE MUST REALISE THAT THE FUNDAMENTAL CHANGES IN SOCIETY SINCE THE WAR—

POORPOISE SQUARE COMPREHENSIVE SCH

REQUIRE *NEW* CONCEPTS OF EDUCATION AND SCHOOLS

This modernisation and humanising of school architecture was carried out entirely by the state. Private schools kept to their old buildings as well as their old divisive selection procedures. This adversely affected the state's implementation of **comprehensive schools** and **mixed-ability** secondary teaching.

Neither comprehensive schools nor their buildings achieved the general high quality of the primary sector.

IT'S ONLY RIGHT THAT WE MAKE AVAILABLE TO OUR CHILDREN THE OPPORTUNITIES—

THAT *WE* NEVER HAD

St Vaizey's
PREPARATORY SCHOOL FOR BOYS
PRIVATE

is for Le Corbusier

From the 1930s onwards the most influential architect of the **Modern Movement** was **Le Corbusier**. To most architects Le Corbusier was (and is) high priest, prophet and god rolled into one. They hung on to his every proclamation, received his latest projects with adulation and made endless pilgrimages to his few completed buildings. Le Corbusier *was* the Modern Movement, the equivalent of **Picasso** in painting or **Stravinsky** in music.

Born **Charles Edouard Jeanneret** in 1887, the son of a Calvinist Swiss watchmaker, Le Corbusier built a few houses in his home town of La Chaux de-Fonds in Neo-Classical style, then left to travel to Greece, Turkey, Germany and France.

IS THAT LE CORBUSIER?

NO, THAT'S GOD, HE JUST THINKS HE'S LE CORBUSIER!

In 1913 Le Corbusier settled in **Paris**, then the centre of avant garde art movements such as **Cubism** and **Surrealism**, to which he contributed **Purism.** Purism in both painting and architecture extolled the idea of the pure typical form, evolved through continual refinement, which included not only the classical temple but also the mass-produced everyday artefacts of the industrial society refined by the economics of machine production. A modern architecture developed on these principles would be given respectability and a pedigree, sharing the same universal principles of simplicity, function and reason.

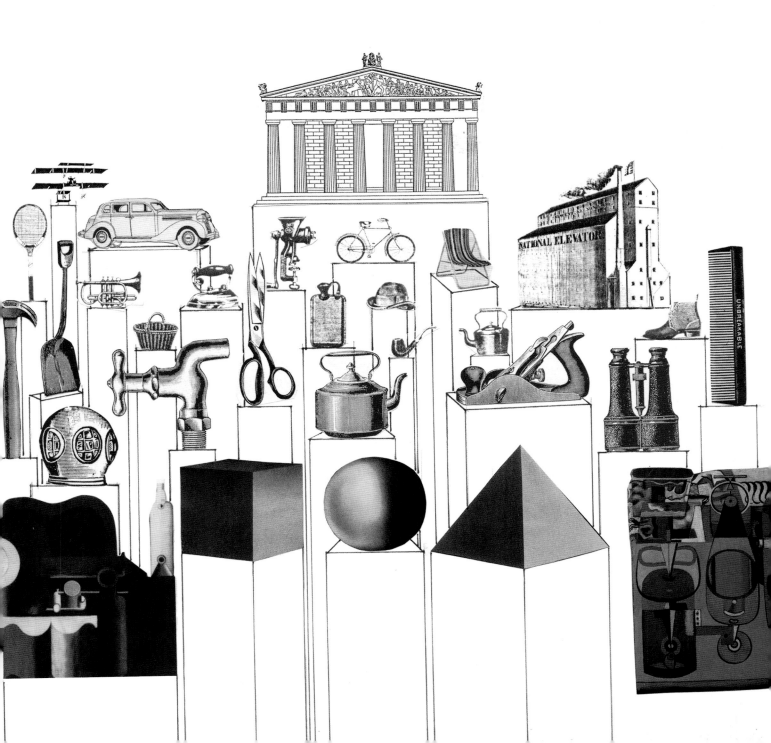

Le Corbusier was a great exponent of the so-called "scientific" method of thinking out each problem afresh. For example, he took the traditional house and analysed it in the light of "cold reason":

Houses traditionally sat on the ground, very old fashioned...

Using modern methods of construction the house could be raised up on legs (**pilotis**), allowing more ground space.

Pitched (sloping) roofs "wasted" space. Flat roofs provided extra space for a garden, saving space on the ground.

Houses had small vertical windows. Modern construction enabled them to be in long strips wrapped round corners.

Since heavy brick walls were replaced by a concrete frame, outside walls could be designed in random Purist patterns.

Internal walls did not need to support the roof so the plan had free-standing elements like an abstract painting.

IT'S OUR CUBE ROOTS

Le Corbusier first put these ideas into practice in the 1920s, designing houses for wealthy art connoisseurs in the leafy Paris suburbs. Interiors were free-flowing interlocking spaces using primary (Purist) colours; exteriors had white-painted walls of cement rendered over breeze blocks (a traditional Continental technique) and steel windows.

Le Corbusier considered that houses should be treated as consumer products, to be wholly prefabricated in factories like cars. Mass-produced homes would roll off the conveyor belts like **Citroen** automobiles, solving the housing problem at a stroke. This idea has obsessed architects ever since (see *I is for Industrial*).

Le Corbusier's best-known pronouncement was that *a house is a machine for living in,* which has been interpreted to mean that a dwelling should be purely functional. In fact Le Corbusier was inspired by *images* of machines, particularly ocean liners, and drew on these to create a new style. His houses were intended to *look* like machines; each part was articulated like the components of a mechanical machine, but they were no more functional than houses in any other style.

His best-known house of this period, **The Villa Savoye** outside Paris, has been likened to a "helicopter poised on a Virgilian field", a synthesis of the machine and classical ideals.

Le Corbusier claimed his method was rationalist not aesthetic. But it was rational in the sense of breaking down into constituent parts and he applied it to all areas of design and planning.

For example, he might analyse the window.
The window's function is:
(a) to let light in
(b) to see out of
(c) to let air in.

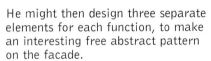

He might then design three separate elements for each function, to make an interesting free abstract pattern on the facade.

In fact, the traditional sliding sash window integrates all these functions simply and economically. Le Corbusier's *dis*-integration methods led architects to over-complicate in the name of innovation, to create problems which were not always there.

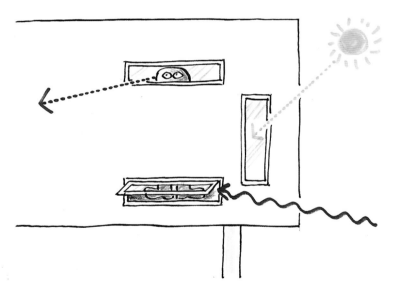

The same system was applied to **town planning** where each function was separated out into **zones** (see also *F is for Futurism*), whereas the character of old towns is usually related to their overlapping functions. But Le Corbusier's planning ideas were to be the most influential of any in the 20th century.

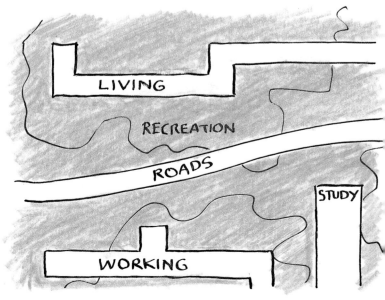

In the 1930s Le Corbusier applied his philosophy of house design to larger structures and at the same time retreated from the ideal of smooth machine-like forms.

Without cornices, sills, overhangs and details the white houses, built by traditional methods, soon cracked, stained and rusted. In his **Swiss student hostel in Paris**, Le Corbusier reverted to stone cladding and random stone walling but, most significantly, the pilotis were sculptured out of raw concrete and left unpainted.

After the Second World War Le Corbusier developed a new design philosophy termed **Brutalism** in English (a misnomer since it derives from the French *brut* meaning raw), whereby the finish of concrete structures is left untreated with the marks of the wooden moulds (**shuttering**) showing. Sheep-like, architects all over the world followed suit.

Le Corbusier now advocated mass housing in the form of self-contained towns on legs, the **Unités**. These were based on the 19th-century philosopher **Charles Fourier**'s failed proposals for "**phalanxes**", self-contained, scientifically planned socialist communes and new cooperative living. The first Unité was built in **Marseilles** for local workers, with internal "streets" (corridors), maisonettes and roof recreation.

It was housing as monumental sculpture, a scaly prehistoric beast, a mega-monastery, but it was inappropriate for its intended users. As the building clearly did not fit people Le Corbusier redesigned people to fit the building, as **Modular man** (and woman), a combination of the **Nietzschean Superman** and the fictional six-foot-tall British detective, **Bulldog Drummond**. Entirely rational, of course.

"Brutalist" Unités were replicated, watered down, by architects all over the world where workers' housing was provided. More often than not the blocks were agents of control rather than liberation.

When Le Corbusier was not trying to be a social engineer he designed some of the most successful, inventive and inspiring buildings of the 20th century.

This was especially true when he served the Church; despite his professed atheism he would work for any client – socialist, fascist, god or devil – who was willing to pay to realise his ideas. The **Monastery of La Tourette**, influenced by Greek towns, and the "organic" form of the **Chapel at Ronchamp**, inspired by a crab shell, evoke timeless spiritual qualities through new forms. They typify the best of Le Corbusier's work – powerful, assertive, plastic, individual, puritan... and made by hand.

Le Corbusier *was* the most inventive of the pioneer modernists. By his death in 1965 he had been the first to explore practically every architectural direction around today.

1. Neo-Classicism
2. Purism
3. Brutalism
4. Linear megastructures
5. Vernacular
6. High Tech
7. Late Modern
8. Post-Modern
9. Eco-houses
10. Deconstruction

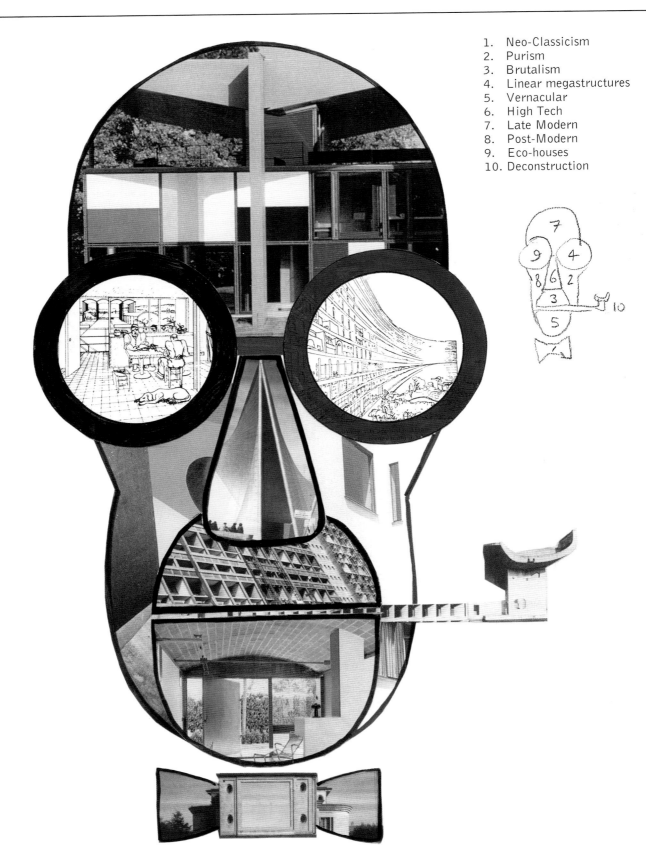

m is for modern

Modern architecture is generally seen to be the particularly rectilinear, machine-aesthetic style of the 20th century, although the term "modern" was used occasionally in other eras, notably the Renaissance.

However, as "modern" architecture developed after the First World War there were numerous configurations and directions including **Futurism, Expressionism** and **Constructivism** as well as **Functionalism** (see also *F is for Futurism*), each a celebration of industrialisation, the defining image of the century.

In the history of art there have always been two basic approaches, **classical** and **romantic,** or the struggle between them, and modern architecture is no exception.

The main characteristics of the two modes are:

Classical
- Imposing order on nature.
- Mathematical, rational.
- Buildings like geometric diagrams.
- Symmetrical.

Romantic
- Integrating with nature.
- Organic, intuitive.
- Buildings like natural forms.
- Asymmetrical.

Of course, these categories are purely for art-historical convenience. There is no pure classicism or romanticism; the one always contains aspects of the other. The classical orders relate to natural forms, the Gothic cathedral has a mathematical order. The same goes for modern architecture.

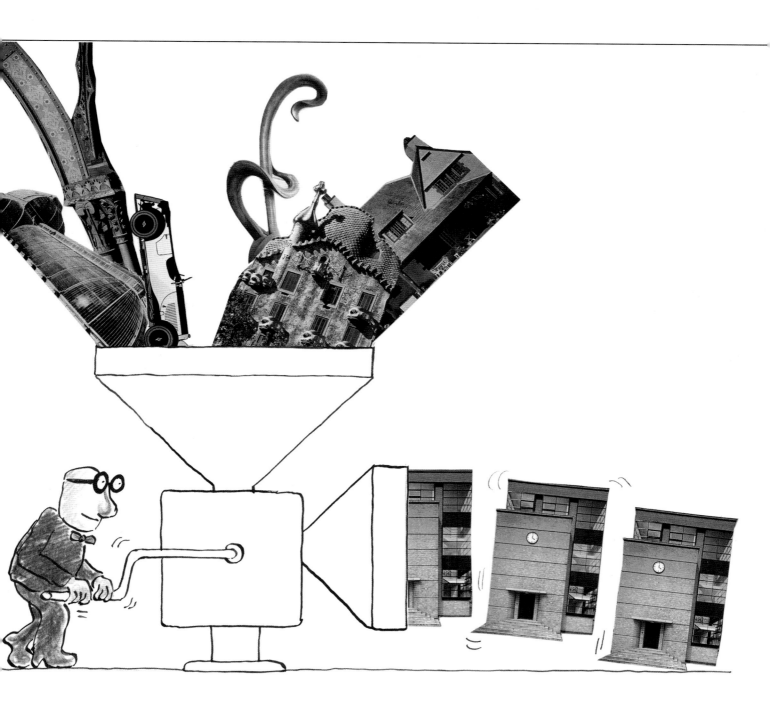

Nothing in art is totally new, and modern architecture evolved from various sources.
On the one hand were the **engineering structures** of the 19th century, which might be
termed the classical or rational input, and machine production as well as the
appearance of the new machines themselves. On the other were the Romantic 19th-
century **Arts and Crafts** movement, inspired by the simplicity of vernacular
buildings, and its successor, **Art Nouveau**, which drew directly on natural forms
rather than classical ideals.

Two examples of **Dutch** housing illustrate alternative directions in modern architecture.

This housing in **Amsterdam**, built in 1917, shows the influence of **Art Nouveau** and local vernacular forms. It is built in brick, an "organic" material, but is generally symmetrical in configuration.

This one-off house in **Utrecht**, built in 1924, is influenced by the **De Stijl** Cubist or Constructivist art movement and consists of "pure" white rectilinear forms and primary colours. It is, however, asymmetrical.

After the Second World War the "rational, mechanistic, abstract, classical" approach dominated. The cube ate the flower. Perhaps because it was easier to achieve as a model for the average architect, perhaps because it just looked more "modern", more "scientific" and more in tune with the age.

  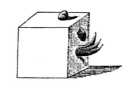 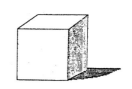

(After Saul Steinberg)

74

The guiding principle of the Modern Movement was "**form follows function**", a rather garbled Darwin-derived theory which implied that if the function was satisfied the appropriate form would emerge automatically without the need for stylistic preconceptions.

However, what developed was another style that *looked* rational, gridded and repetitive like graph paper, as well as seeming "classical" or, rather, "neo-classical".

But the buildings were often far from functional. New materials such as steel, reinforced concrete and glass were used to achieve the look without sufficient understanding of how they would perform.

Steel frames had already been used in buildings but were usually covered up with stone or brick to imitate old styles. Modernists saw this as sham and "dishonest" and considered that the frame should be expressed. "Honest" structural expression was a key requirement of Functionalism.

The **Fagus Shoe Factory** of 1911 was one of the first architect-designed buildings to express the gridded frame but, more importantly, it was also among the first to dissolve the corner. For structural reasons, masonry buildings always had solid corners but now the glass could wrap around them since floors and roof were supported by the steel frame. It was another key element of the new architecture.

HOME SWEET HOME!

One of the main precepts of the Functional style was "truth to materials". It is ironic, then, that the major structural material of the 20th century should be **reinforced concrete**, a highly "unnatural" amalgam of two materials, cement and steel.

The Ancient Romans had used concrete to construct their massive edifices. Using slave labour, it was a quick and cheap substitute for stone and could be faced in stone or brick.

A mixture of sandy earth, lime and water was put into wooden moulds.

When set, the resulting concrete was very tough in **compression**...

but not...

in **tension** (bending).

Concrete was abandoned until the Industrial Revolution developed methods of mass-producing steel in long continuous bars which made it possible to reinforce concrete. It was an ideal marriage: the concrete took care of the compression and embedded steel reinforcing bars dealt with the tension.

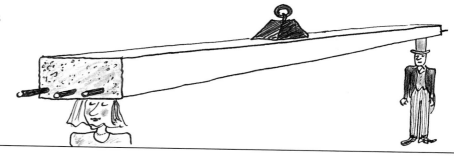

Reinforced concrete is a highly versatile material. It can be used to construct free-flowing curves or shells, cantilevers, vast spans or posts and beams and is a cheaper alternative to steel frames as well as being inherently fireproof.

The administrative centre of the new capital of **Brasilia** (right), the capital of Brazil since 1960, exploits both these qualities.

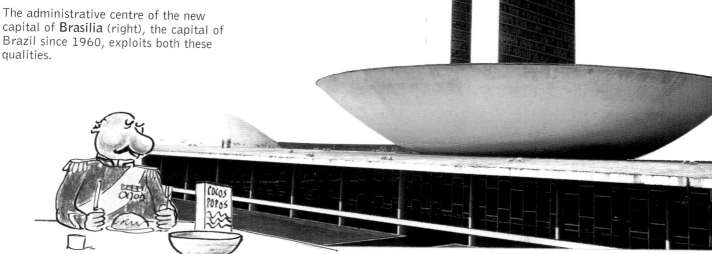

The third principal component of the Functional style is the **glass** wall.

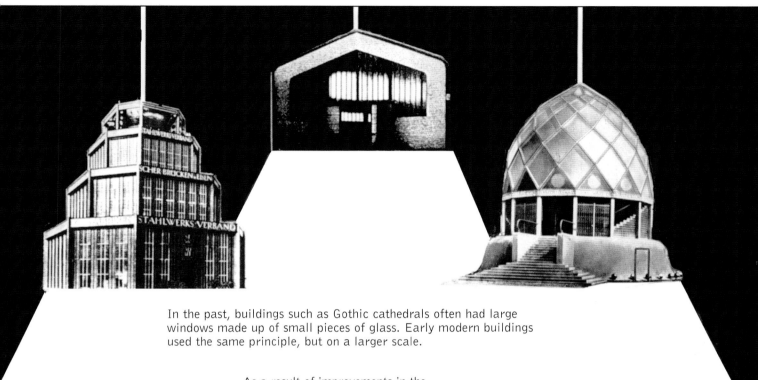

In the past, buildings such as Gothic cathedrals often had large windows made up of small pieces of glass. Early modern buildings used the same principle, but on a larger scale.

As a result of improvements in the manufacture of plate glass, which can now be made in huge sheets, outside walls can be almost entirely translucent, dissolving the barrier between inside and outside and giving the impression of infinite space.

Another essential ingredient of the Functional style was the **flat roof**.

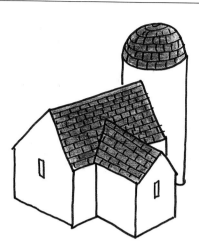

The geometry of the traditional sloping roof or dome usually limited the form of buildings to combinations of simple rectangles.

But the development of the modern flat roof, covered in asphalt or plastic, enabled the plan to be any shape.

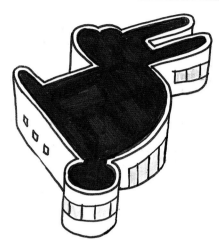

What was lost was storage space, space to hide water tanks or plant and, in rainy countries, the ability to drain water off quickly.

During the hegemony of the Functionalist or Machine Aesthetic style from the 1950s until the 1970s, architects assumed the role of missionaries, spreading the gospel to those with power and money. Local cultures, traditions and social networks were irrelevant and outdated. There would, as Le Corbusier said, "be one single building type for all nations and climates".

This hegemony ended during the late 1970s as part of a disillusionment with modernism in all the arts which had developed after the Second World War in response to social and political change. The death of Functionalism was proclaimed as **Post-Modernism** emerged (see also *S is for Styles*).

There was desire to return to the *art* of architecture, and to the clear language and symbolism of historic building forms. But this was either impossible where vast building types were required, or it ended up with essentially modern blocks being dressed up in bits of neohistoric detail. Back to square one. It was this kind of dressing up of modern structures in archaic clothing that the Modern Movement had reacted to in the first place.

In effect, architects trawled back over the history of the Modern Movement and rediscovered the alternatives to Functionalism such as **Constructivism** or **Organic** architecture (qv). At the same time building technology, assisted by the information revolution, had improved, enabling the old problems associated with modern buildings to be tempered. After the short-lived **Post-Modern** phase, modern architecture dominated once more, but now it employed advanced technology in a **Late-Modern** or **Baroque-Modern** manner. The cube and the flower were coming together.

n is for neo-classical

Neo-Classicism is the revival of the architecture of **Ancient Greece** and **Rome**. This first occurred in 15th-century **Italy** where, as is usually the case, a new power elite spawned a "new" architecture.

In the city-state of **Florence**, moneylending was elevated to banking. Powerful European kings ran their countries like big businesses and needed capital to finance enterprises, hire armies and colonise continents. Florentine banker-families like the **Medicis**, **Strozzis** and **Pazzis** grew immensely rich, ran the city, appointed themselves princes and patronised the arts, vying with each other in splendour and ostentation.

They desired a break with the past, or rather the power of the Church, and looked back to the period when Italy had been great, the Roman era, for a secular architecture to proclaim the dominance of the new middle classes over the state and the Church. The study of classical culture was thus practically applied in the Italian power centres where man and the world, not God and heaven, were at the centre of the universe: the **Renaissance.**

Since they knew little of Rome and still less of Greece, Florentine architects were mainly influenced by the **Romanesque** style, of which there were many examples in the city. They also studied the remains of Roman temples or villas which had been ignored during the Middle Ages, though they did not copy them cold but employed the language of classical architecture creatively, using **Gothic** (qv) technology which had become relatively sophisticated during the construction of the great cathedrals.

So the ingredients of the new Renaissance style were the Romanesque and the Gothic which had been developed by the Church; fortified medieval buildings developed by the state; and classical principles.

Florentine banker-families expanded their medieval town houses into palaces, statements of their importance, now adorned with classical elements, arched windows, floors defined by horizontal bands (**string courses**), carved stonework (rustication) and large overhanging moulded tops (**cornices**). These palaces were urban, located in dangerous narrow streets, and consequently were fortress-like on the outside. Later, the interior of the palaces had a contrasting character. A central court with arcades gave light and air to the rooms as in a **Roman villa**, with living accommodation on the first floor (**piano nobile**). A haven from the hostile exterior world.

Renaissance architects were no longer builders or craftsmen as in the Gothic era, but scholars or artists engaged in "design concepts" communicated in drawings and writings which were influenced by the books of the Roman architect **Vitruvius** who had laid down precepts for the practice of classical architecture.

No longer tied to guilds, they were "free" to sell their "genius" to the highest bidder. The Renaissance spawned the **Universal Man** superstar who could turn his hand to anything: painting, sculpture, science, poetry, astronomy... even architecture.

Classical orders and elements were used by Renaissance architects like a variable kit of parts, both externally and internally. This was a feature of Neo-classicism since...

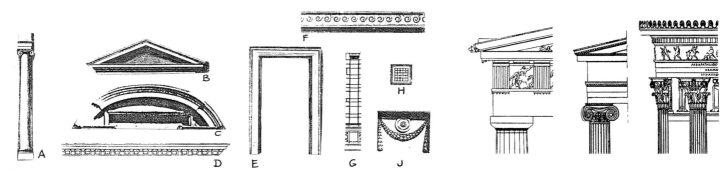

This kit of parts could be used to compose buildings large...

or small...

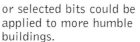

or selected bits could be applied to more humble buildings.

Since the classical orders evolved from primitive buildings (see *T is for Temples*), and their details derived from plant or natural forms, when used well they established both human scale and evocations of nature.

Despite the Church's hostility to the humanist ideals of the Renaissance, early examples of the new architecture were applied to churches. The best-known examples are the dome of **Florence's Gothic Cathedral** by **Brunelleschi**, a feat of Gothic engineering applied to a dome form, and the Florentine Gothic church of **Santa Maria Novella**, where **Alberti** completed a Romanesque front using classical elements. Today you can hardly see the join.

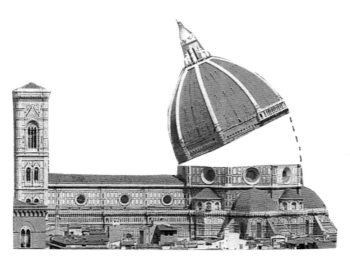

Andrea Palladio had the greatest influence of the Late Renaissance architects. He advocated a return to a cool, refined yet practical architecture designed according to the laws of nature and the order of the universe as embodied in mathematical proportion.

He extended the idea of the building reflecting the elements of the human body (**biomorphism**).

- The building should be symmetrical from the front like the body with a central "**axis**" (the spine).

- The more important elements should be in the middle, like the head, brain, eyes, nose, mouth (entrance), etc.

- Elements on the outside should reflect the structure (like skin over bones).

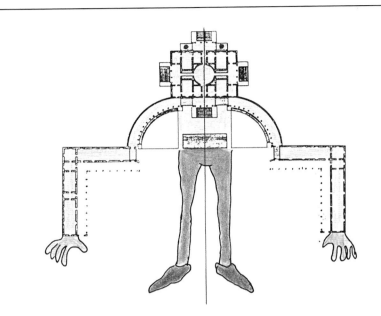

Palladio designed a series of country villas for the landed gentry around Venice according to these principles. He assumed that Roman villas had been like small temples so he attached temple fronts to the traditional rural farmhouse model while integrating the building into its landscaped setting.

By the 16th century the centre of banking had moved to **Germany** and the **Netherlands**. The invention of **printing** had spread the ideas of the Renaissance all over Europe.

The Pope still had influence, but keeping up with kings was expensive. Finance for huge projects, especially **St Peter's** in Rome (started by **Bramante** and **Michelangelo**), was raised by selling indulgences, fake relics or positions in high places.

In Germany, the new urban rich objected to the Church's dominance – it hampered business. Prompted by this and the corruption of the Pope, parts of the German Church severed themselves from Rome to pursue their own brand of Christianity and **Protestantism** was born. This revolt spread throughout northern Europe and resulted in the **Reformation**.

Here, the Renaissance first took the form of classical elements grafted onto the local Gothic styles, a symbol of the encroachment of the new culture on the old.

France's invasions of Italy under **Francis I** exposed the French to Renaissance art and they imported Italian architects. The **French chateaux** in the hunting areas along the Loire valley slowly absorbed the classical style. But while they were no longer the fortified castles of old they maintained medieval corner towers, turrets and high-pitched roofs.

In **England**, which had grown into a world power under **Elizabeth I**, aristocrats built huge country houses which combined medieval and classical elements as well as gigantic windows, first developed in Gothic cathedrals but now in classical proportions. This symbolised both the transfer of power from Church to laity and the country's open confidence in the stability of the new social order.

Just as Gothic architecture had grown more decorated, the High Renaissance of the 16th century became bolder, more confident, sculptured and "mannered".

The classical rules were bent, distorted and juggled until they were almost dispensed with as **High Renaissance** evolved into first the **Baroque** and then **Rococo**. The orders were employed in free compositions and individualised statements. Heights of columns were varied, curved pediments were placed inside triangular ones, play was made with scrolls and niches.

The Reformation had involved a considerable loss of power and influence for the Catholic Church, and the growth of rational science had disproved some of its fundamental dogmas, particularly that the world was the centre of the universe. But it had succumbed to the classical style and now it employed the High Renaissance as part of the **Counter Reformation** mounted by the fiercely zealous **Jesuit** order. Their base was the new church of **Il Gesù** in Rome, by **Vignola**. Humanist influences brought reforms, but religious intolerance resulted in the persecution of Protestants, particularly in France and Spain.

DISTORT, BEND, STRETCH... IT'S THE LATEST STYLE !

The church of **Il Gesù** demonstrates the artificiality of historical categories. Is it **Late Renaissance**, **Mannerist** or **Early Baroque** – the **Baroque** being the style for Church and state from the mid-17th to the 18th century.

By the 17th century, **France** had emerged as Europe's most powerful state, centralised under an **absolute monarch** with a self-proclaimed divine right to rule. The King *was* the state and he regulated not only business, but also the arts and sciences by means of **Royal Academies**. And a new breed of architect was born: the official court adviser who designed palaces, churches and public buildings. The king's total power was expressed in vast Baroque palaces with formal gardens extending out to infinity – the infinity he owned.

During the Counter-Reformation, Italy embarked on a programme of church building which exploited Baroque ostentation as a deliberate contrast to Protestant austerity.

The Roman Catholic Church had adopted some Renaissance ideas together with its architecture, but in its churches it moulded them to its traditional structure.

The "centralised" plan, particularly in the form of a circle, was idealised by Renaissance architects as symbolising man at the centre of the universe. In church planning this clashed with the medieval liturgical requirement for a nave to separate the congregation from the mystery of God.

The Baroque solution was the **oval**, a dynamic (or distorted) compromise between the focused triumphalism of the cross shape and the calm inner harmony of the circle.

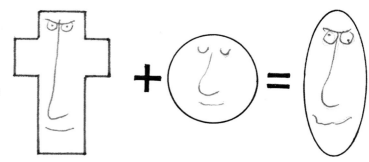

In Rome the architects **Bernini**, suave and sophisticated, and **Borromini**, fanatical and introverted, vied with each other in designing Baroque churches based on oval plans.

San Carlo by Borromini unifies its classical elements in a revolutionary manner by fusing them into an undulating, flowing, plastic whole.

San Andrea by Bernini manipulates classical elements to achieve a dynamic integration of sculpture, painting and architecture, rather like a stage set.

In the 18th century there was a return to a fundamental classicism – a reaction to Baroque excess, and appropriate to the **Age of Reason** where science was the measure of everything and taste became simple and refined.

The Age of Reason ended with the bourgeois revolutions in **America** and **France** which laid down the foundations for the modern world and modern architecture. British imperialism in America and absolute monarchy in France, with their power to tax, were repressive obstacles to the expansion of free-market capitalism.

Appropriate to the new "scientifically" run states, the regimes adopted classical architecture and a return to Greek and Roman styles. The **capitol**, the **triumphal arch** and the **pantheon** were the models glorifying the new democratic republics.

Nineteenth-century **nationalism** (see *V is for Vernacular*) was in part a reaction to "foreign" Neo-Classicism, but the latter resurfaced after the First World War and was adopted by totalitarian regimes in **Italy**, **Germany** and the **USSR** in a "stripped", overblown version.

(Cartoon by Osbert Lancaster)

The Modern Movement felt it had buried Neo-Classicism for good. It was seen as the architecture of repression and dictator power. But like **Antæus**, the Greek god who drew power from the earth, Neo-Classicism seems indestructable. It has returned as part of the Post-Modern trawling of the past to find alternatives to Functionalism and even been applied to gargantuan public-sector housing developments with "people's" columns 10 storeys high.

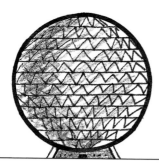 # O is for organic

Before industrialisation, all buildings could be said to be made from "organic" materials or, rather, "dead" organic materials.

Trees provide habitats...

are cut up for timber...

to build huts and shrines...
(See also *T is for Temples*)

to become transmuted into stone (dead fossils).

Organic architecture is defined by various concepts:

There is an inherent, biological impulse to build in all living things.

There is an analogy between human and animal forms and buildings.

Ornament and/or the whole building should be derived from plant forms.

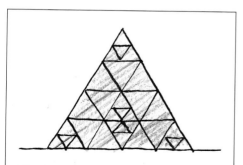

The biological analogy that the parts should be in harmony with the whole.

The idea that, as in nature, form evolves to follow (serve) function.

The structural principles of natural form can be applied to buildings.

Although birds, ants, bees and many insects build, few mammals do (beavers and badgers are the best known exceptions), and usually seek natural shelters such as caves and trees, or burrow holes. People's impulse to build may not therefore be inherent but more to do with mind, observation and imitation.

All historic buildings, whether preclassical, classical, medieval, Gothic or oriental, had organic references or analogies with symbolic, stylised ornament derived from animal and plant forms. Primitive buildings might imitate beehives or nests.

Since the **ancient Egyptian** temples and before, buildings and building plans have related to the human body (**anthropomorphism**). We still say buildings "lie", "rise up", have "fronts" and "backs" and "faces" (**facades**), "silhouettes", "profiles" and windows which "look out". Historically, buildings had "heads" (**domes, spires**) and "feet" (**plinths, bases**) as well as "wings" (**zoomorphism**). Towers may be "phallic", domes "breast-like", entrances "vaginal" and rooms "womb-like".

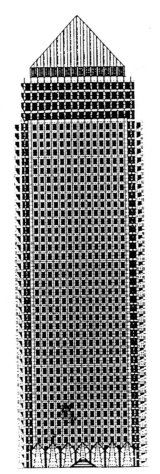

The **Art Nouveau** movement in art and architecture in the late 19th century rejected Neo-Classical models and sought inspiration to create a new style from observing nature directly.

Unlike its precursor, the **Arts and Crafts** movement, Art Nouveau looked forward in the spirit of the *fin-de-siècle,* leaving behind the old for the new, and exploited the new possibilities of materials such as cast iron, glass and concrete. The free-form curve was its hallmark: the dynamic stem structure of plants and buds, lilies, sunflowers, tree roots, the swan and the peacock. Its sources and influences were extensive, for those who could afford it.

A WHIFF OF ORGANIC SENSUALITY...

A DASH OF JAPANESE... A TWIST OF CELTIC...

A SLIVER OF BAROQUE... A PINCH OF MOORISH EXOTIC

GIVE IT ALL A GOOD STIR AND ...

NOTHING?!

AH MY FRIEND YOU'VE FORGOTTEN THE ESSENTIAL INGREDIENT

LASHINGS AND LASHINGS OF MONEY — ET VOILA!

L'ART NOUVEAU RICH.!

Guimard's famous **Paris Metro** stations (1899–1900) demonstrate the new art in the service of the new democratic society and new industrial prosperity. Sinuous plant forms in cast iron, and leaf-like glass canopies, marked the entrances to the new rapid, underground public transport system.

Gaudí's buildings in **Barcelona** fused organic-based form and structure as in the **Casa Batlló** of 1906. The roof represents St George, Barcelona's patron saint, slaying the dragon of Spain — a symbol of **Catalonia**'s desire for independence. The death-mask balconies and the bone-like structure symbolise Catalan martyrs.

The principal exponent of organic architecture, and America's best-known architect, was **Frank Lloyd Wright** (1867–1959), who represented a continuous link between the Modern Movement and its 19th-century origins.

Wright aimed to create an essentially American modern architecture, firmly rooted in indigenous vernacular forms based on those of **Native Americans** and **Mayans**, or pioneers' wooden structures, as well as **Japanese** culture and its direct relationship to nature.

His mystical romanticism also stemmed from the great American 19th century writers such as **Thoreau** and **Emerson,** and especially the poet **Walt Whitman** and his celebration of the American landscape, individual freedom and the spirit of radical pioneering.

Wright's concept of **organic architecture** involved buildings that were both at one with, and inspired by, nature.

He associated all great architecture with plant and animal forms and saw eternal laws and a correlation between form and function in the relationship of the parts to the whole. Following his mentor **Louis Sullivan**'s philosophy he sought truth in nature's fundamental *principles* as opposed to surface *appearance*.

These principles were developed in the so-called **Prairie Houses**, the main elements being:

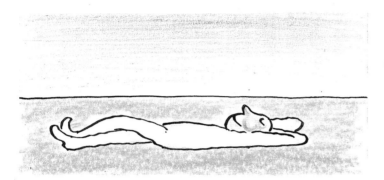

Horizontality
Wright saw the horizontal line as symbolising and evoking oneness with nature, as opposed to the vertical line which symbolises man's domination of the natural world.

Sympathy with the site
Buildings should be designed to blend with the natural elements of the site. From Japanese temples he learnt the art of merging building and landscape.

Domestic symbolism
Houses should retain the traditional elements that evoke home, welcome, warmth and protection, including low pitched roofs, projecting eaves, low ceilings and generous fireplaces at the centre.

Truth to materials
"Natural" materials such as brick, stone, wood and tile should be used untreated and not forced into shapes which are against their inherent nature.

Open planning
Internally there should be no box-like rooms, but free-flowing, interconnecting volumes symbolising "infinite space" and extending outwards into the grounds with no barriers between inside and out.

Character
Each house would be designed according to these fundamental organic principles and the unique nature of the site, rather than any predetermined style. There should be as many styles as there are people.

However, Wright's Prairie Houses, built up to 1910, were not located in wide open spaces but in the **Chicago** suburbs. They were to house not free-ranging pioneers, but affluent Midwest businessmen who had profited from the industrial expansion of the city.

FROM HERE YOU CAN SEE THE WIDE OPEN SPACES OF THE SUPERMARKET PARKING LOT !

The **Robie House** of 1909 is the best known. Here Wright exploded the tight European Arts and Crafts brick box into a free arrangement of dynamic, linear, expanding spaces. The low-pitched roofs hover protectively and reach out to encompass the surroundings, although these seemingly long cantilevered roofs are in fact built up on reinforced concrete slabs, not exactly "truth to materials".

Even more famous among the hundreds of houses Wright designed is "**Falling Water**" (1936), built outside **Philadelphia** for the department store tycoon Edgar Kaufmann.

This stunning house sits on a rock above a waterfall where architecture and nature literally fuse.

Here Wright accepts reinforced concrete, hardly an "organic" material and one that does not exactly blend with the natural surroundings (though he did originally want it covered in gold leaf).

Another example of idealistic philosophy giving way to pragmatism.

Up to 1910, Wright's work had a great influence in Europe, but for more than 20 years after that he was then rejected by hard-line modernists for his romanticism, anti-collectivism, use of traditional materials and ornament. He was seen as the last of the 19th-century pioneers.

In fact Wright's use of modern technology was often far in advance of the Europeans. He was among the first to use the cantilever, central heating, air conditioning, double glazing, open-planned kitchens, underfloor heating and carports and, because he combined these with traditional materials, his buildings often avoided the poor internal environments and weathering problems of the Functionalists.

Although always seeking to design horizontally, Wright did not turn down commisions for high buildings and attempted to apply his organic principles to them. The **Johnson Wax** office tower and research laboratories in **Racine** (1936–1948) typify his approach, drawing inspiration from organic structures while using new technology and an innovatory application of traditional materials such as brick. Externally the buildings are in the **Art Deco** (see *U is for the USA*) streamlined style of a juke box, Cadillac or electric guitar.

The office building is composed of concrete columns based on a mushroom or lily-pad form while the tower is akin to a tree: its basement is the roots, its service core the trunk and its cantilevered floors the branches. (See also the pagoda in *J is for Japan*.)

But Wright professed opposition to the industrial city and when he built in one, as at Johnson Wax, he often shut out the surroundings behind solid walls with top lighting.

His most famous postwar building is the **Guggenheim Museum** in **New York** (1957), which is in the form of a spiral, another organic form, and deliberately in opposition to the city's rectilinear grid.

Years earlier Wright had designed a hotel in Tokyo which had survived the great earthquake of 1923 because he had made the structure flexible and capable of accommodating earth movement. He now declared that the Guggenheim would cope with a nuclear attack by bouncing like a spring, presumably all the way to his beloved Midwest. This has yet to be tested.

Long before Brunelleschi's famous dome for Florence Cathedral was inspired by the structure of an egg, buildings have related to organic form.

In the 20th century there were airports like birds, bridges like dinosaur skeletons, opera houses and restaurants like flowers, hockey rinks and stations like leaves, cathedrals like termite nests, sports stadia like jellyfish, cultural centres like armadillos, houses like beehives or genitals and so on.

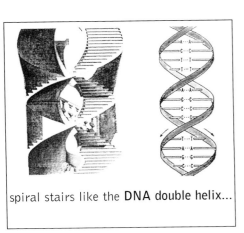

spiral stairs like the **DNA double helix**...

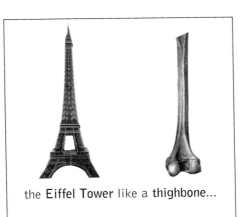

the **Eiffel Tower** like a **thighbone**...

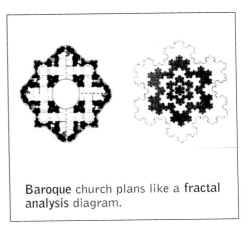

Baroque church plans like a **fractal analysis** diagram.

But in the latter half of the 20th century, advances in **molecular biology** and **chemical analysis** showed that not just the forms, but the structural and material *principles* of organisms could be applied to buildings. Structures are of **fibrous cellular** (animals and plants) or **inert granular** (eggs or shells) nature, often evolved to provide maximum economy of material under the principle of **strong yet light.**

The humble blade of grass, though thin, gains strength by being folded, giving rise to the idea of corrugation in building structures.

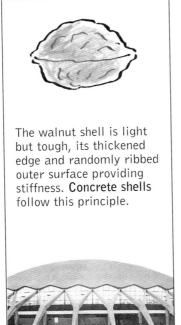

The walnut shell is light but tough, its thickened edge and randomly ribbed outer surface providing stiffness. **Concrete shells** follow this principle.

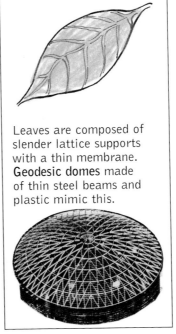

Leaves are composed of slender lattice supports with a thin membrane. **Geodesic domes** made of thin steel beams and plastic mimic this.

The threads in a spider's web are fragile singly but strong as a network. **Tensile steel cable** structures follow this principle, light yet strong in combination.

The application of organic form has now extended into the discipline of **biomimetics**, a combination of biology and engineering, which studies not merely static structures but metamorphosis and shape change. Perhaps truly organic buildings will be feasible in the future?

is for politics

Every piece of architecture is a political statement as well as an aesthetic experience. Any building operation requires relatively huge resources and, historically, monumental buildings expressed the dominance of the ruling elite, raised up above and dominating the habitats of the general community.

WE OWNED 99% OF THE WEALTH OF THE NATION

WE OWNED 90% OF THE WEALTH OF THE NATION

WE OWN 85% OF THE WEALTH OF THE NATION

But as one ruling elite was replaced by another or its power diminished, the buildings became historic monuments, appreciated for their aesthetic qualities and targeted by tourists. If they were symbols of oppression, this is now forgotten.

Imperialist dictatorship run by military style junta based on slave labour.

Plutocracy governed by corrupt and bigoted cleric class exploiting mass ignorance.

Society dominated by oligarchic mafia of murderers, usurers and torturers.

Paradoxically, the all-powerful rulers of Ancient Egypt, Rome, the Middle Ages or the Renaissance often produced architecture of sublime beauty, and it was not until the 20th century that state bureaucracies or private capital were often typified by brutal, arid or mundane buildings which destroyed much-loved old towns and cities in the name of progress or profit.

Yet these same loved old towns and cities were built by private enterprise or authoritarian power. Why then does this so often fail today?

It is partly due to the scale of modern construction (more buildings built in the last 50 years than in the last 500), the death of handmade craftsmanship and the lack of patronage, the aims and motives of those who commission buildings. In the past the patron was an emperor, pope, prince, king or entrepreneur who desired a monument of high quality and who was invariably educated in matters of taste, talked the language of design and chose the best architects.

The Modern Movement set out to serve the needs of the whole of society but soon reverted to the traditional role of building new monuments for new elites, committees of politicians or accountants and boards of directors in the public or private sectors who were more interested in quantity, rock-bottom economy or control, than architectural quality.

Between the two world wars, totalitarian regimes deliberately used architecture as an instrument of oppression (see *N is for Neo-Classical*), not only in the erection of vast stadia, monuments or elite party palaces, but also in the death camps, most of which were designed by architects.

The problem is that architecture, being fundamentally an art form, has no moral imperative. Doctors are committed to save life and lawyers to pursue justice, and can be brought to book if they fail to do so, but art has no moral aim. It can be disturbing, terrifying or shocking as well as inspiring or enhancing.
The Modern Movement had also promoted the notion of the architect as an apolitical technocrat applying objective reasoning to building and urban design without considering the social context.

Most architects, however, set out to improve the environment and design buildings which are pleasing and comfortable. But they are always answerable to the client who pays for the construction and who may have other agendas.

Architects who professed to have a "social conscience" worked in the public sector designing buildings for the welfare state. But here they were directed by state bureaucracies which were often out of tune with the needs of the clientele and had a vested interest in building "monuments" to the housing or health problem – visible evidence of political action despite their inappropriateness.

In the private sector, International Style modern architecture was adopted by international-style land speculators to provide brand images for office headquarters or monuments to consumerism, as well as luxury flats or hotels. Such profit-led developers were usually unconcerned about their environmental impact, had the power and influence to get planning consent and had no shortage of architects willing to collude with them.

Like most professionals, architects are supposed to be impartial and without vested interests but they are inevitably seen as the client's agents: at worst hired guns for those with power who patronise, dictate to or discount the mass of people in society...

or, like road engineers, being blind to, or unconcerned about, the effects of their proposals.

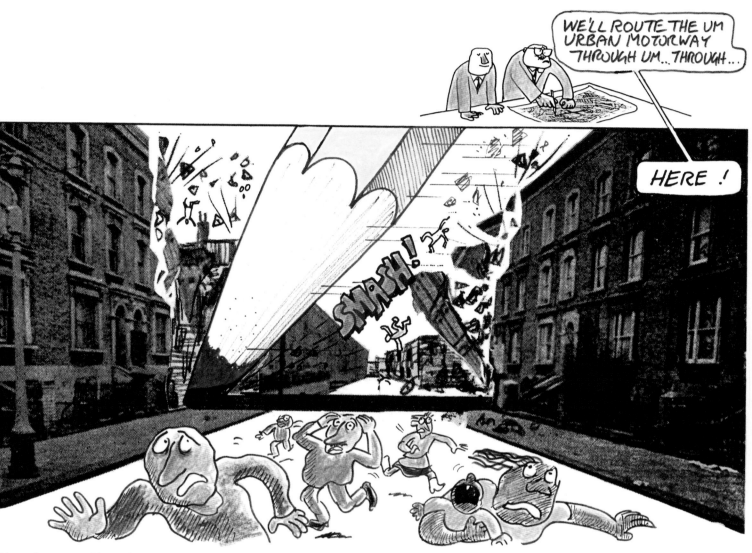

Since the 1960s ideas about "participation" or "consultation" in terms of communities or the recipients of public-sector buildings have been floated but have rarely been successful, or they are adopted as window dressing to give schemes spurious political credibility.

Without power, resources and technical knowhow people usually have to defer to the wishes of those who have them – those whom architects will continue to serve until society legislates otherwise.

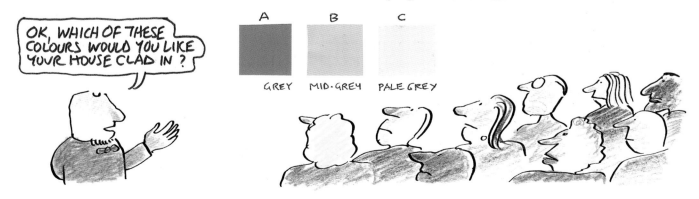

The post-war period saw the emergence of two nuclear superpowers, the **USA** and its **Western European** dependent states, and the **USSR** and its satellites.

While Russia and its satellites adhered to the stripped classical style, the West embraced modern architecture, or its strictly rectilinear version, for developments in both the welfare state and US-style commercial sectors.

The poverty-stricken "third" or "developing" world, led by **China**, continued to be exploited for its cheap goods and labour.

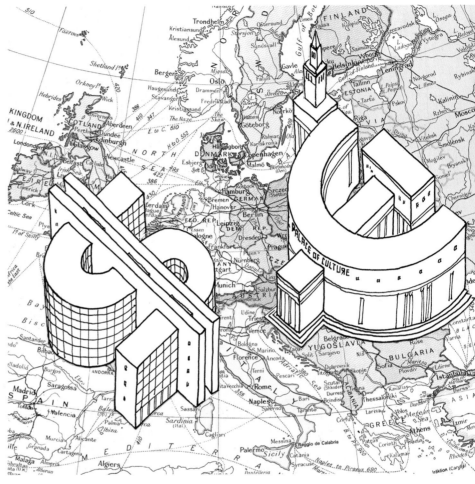

The **United Nations** complex, built in **New York** in 1950 so that nations would talk rather than make war, demonstrates how modern architectural symbolism can be inappropriate. The debating chamber, the *raison d'être* of the UN, is dominated by the administration tower (of **Babel**?), symbol of the bureaucratic nature of modern political power.

The last decade of the 20th century saw the collapse of monolithic communism in the USSR and Eastern Europe and the deconstruction of the empire into its constituent nation-state parts.

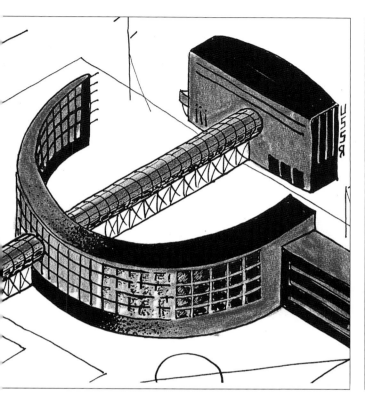 

The end of eastern totalitarian communism has seen the emergence of the **United States** as the most powerful country in the world, economically, militarily and politically. American financial and industrial multinational giants now operate globally, building factories or headquarters or cultural centres at will while dictating conditions to local governments or "showing the natives how to do it".

The end of the 20th century was characterised by the global economy, the fall or decline of state socialism and the problems of population growth and an impoverished Third World.

Architects, as ever, serve wealth and power, and the stars of the profession are busy designing ever larger and more exotic monuments to neocolonial **multinationalism** in world financial centres or where labour is cheap and politics repressive. Capital operates internationally, while labour and politics are static and national.

Not just the clients but the very buildings themselves are multinational. The **Hong Kong and Shanghai Bank** in Hong Kong, for a time the costliest building in the world, is made of high-tech components manufactured in advanced industrialised countries all over the world, from Germany to New Zealand. The site could be anywhere.

In the West, the decline of a mass industrial workforce and the growth of a service-providing middle class has seen the diminution of state welfare and an increasing reliance on the private purchase of healthcare, housing and education, together with the privatisation of transport, infrastructures and urban renewal.

This process has left a residual "underclass" who may be unemployed, homeless, disenfranchised or on social benefits. Particularly in inner city areas this has led to problems of crime and unrest and an obsession with security and fortification. The open society that the Modern Movement designed for seems to be a thing of the past.

1950s "SLUMS"

1960s "BRAVE NEW WORLD"

1970s "VANDALISM"

1980s "REHABILITATION"

1990s "YUPPIEFICATION"

THE MILLENNIUM?

The so-called "end of ideology" has meant that architecture is no longer linked to any social programme of mass state housing, hospital or school building. A plurality of modern architectural directions (see *S is for Style*) serves a variety of public and (mostly) private building types.

is for qualifications

All buildings, however humble, have an architect (literally "chief builder"), the person who makes strategic decisions before construction is commenced (see *D is for Design*), whether this be the person in charge of a homeless family putting up a shack in a shanty town or an international superstarchitect.

Today architecture is an academic discipline and a profession, but in previous eras the architects of large-scale monumental buildings might come from various walks of life and add design to their other responsibilities.

In **Mesopotamia** and **Egypt** they were the ruling priest class...

In **Ancient Greece** they might be monumental sculptors...

In **Roman** times they were usually military engineers...

In the **Middle Ages** they were monks or master masons...

In the **Renaissance** they were artists, sculptors or scientists...

In the **18th century** they were often gentlemen amateurs.

But by the 19th century economic growth, advances in building technology, the onset of building regulations and the proliferation of new social building types such as hospitals, town halls, fire stations, libraries, gaols, schools and housing meant that the practice of architectural design could no longer be an amateur pastime.

Architects formed themselves into a **profession** so that, as artists not tradesmen, they were distinguished from surveyors or engineers (who formed their own professions), builders and developers.

This inevitably led to examinations for qualification and registration, and eventually to schools of architecture where the constituent disciplines and theories could be taught. Until then, prospective architects paid to be "articled" or apprenticed to offices which were supposed to instruct them in the art and practice of the profession.

From the early 19th century, the most pervasive method of architectural education was that known as the **beaux arts** system, from the school in **Paris** set up by **Napoleon** in 1819. Its influence lasted until the 1960s.

Beaux-arts students imaginary projects on paper were characterised by their vast scale, strict symmetry, elemental composition and the Neo-Classical or Neo-Baroque style.

Modernist critics in the 20th century maintained that the system was too academic, out of touch with the real world, separated architecture from its practical craft base and had degenerated into a rigid and inflexible rule-obsessed dogma.

Pioneer modernists like Le Corbusier detested the beaux-arts system and sought alternative educational principles based on science and new technology.

In 1919, **Walter Gropius** set up the **Bauhaus** in the existing Arts and Crafts School in the old town of **Weimar**, seat of the new postwar German republic.

The original aim of the Bauhaus was to reunite the arts and crafts in the creation of a new architecture and to institute learning by doing as opposed to the beaux-arts learning by academic instruction, fostering inate abilities rather than inculcating methods, and eradicating all previous teaching and preconceptions.

In some form this was to influence modern architectural courses from then on.

First there was a six-month preliminary "cleansing" foundation course...

then three years of instruction in crafts such as metalwork or ceramics...

followed by architecture and research for a vague unspecified period.

Local political opposition and internal rifts led to a move to **Dessau,** a dissolution of the original aims as Gropius embraced machine production and standardisation (which superseded handicraft) which and a return to the division between practical and academic instruction. The latter was dominated by the notion of **basic design** as an attempt to apply scientific methods to art. It was thought that an art product could be broken down into (and hence built up from) its constituent parts like molecules – the basic elements of design – which invariably turned out to be the sphere, the cone and the cube (or square, circle and triangle).

The Bauhaus became famous for its supposedly machine-made artefacts like the tubular steel chair (inspired by a bicycle), rather than its architectural graduates.

But the new school building designed by Gropius and made possible by the ending of the economic recession, advanced the Functionalist style considerably, with a plan-form like a free abstract composition, large areas of glass, white bands and flat roofs. The innovatory building that bridges the road in fact connected the now separate schools of craft and theory.

The school was closed by the Nazis in 1932.

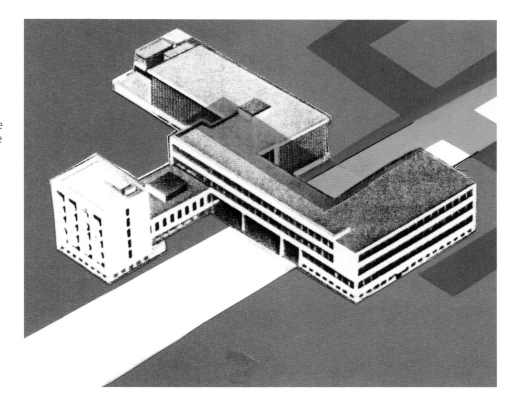

After the Second World War, Bauhaus-influenced systems of architectural education gradually replaced the beaux-art historicist method, and architecture split off from the old arts and crafts schools to be introduced as a department in universities or technical colleges.

In the 1960s and 1970s, the ever-increasing amount of technical, scientific, legal, environmental and social know-how required to practise architecture led schools to neglect traditional subjects such as aesthetics or history and concentrate on architecture's rational side.

Information and knowledge usurped understanding and creativity, while students became increasingly politicised and questioning of the architect's role in society.

In the 1980s, under the influence of Post-Modern ideas, there was a reaction to the exclusively technical view of education and traditional subjects were reintroduced. Now given an academic pedigree as a university discipline, as well as the additional funding such status attracted, architecture courses in Britain adopted a three-part system:

Part One. Degree. Three years
A general course in theory, design and history enabling graduates to proceed to other related disciplines.

Part Two. Diploma. Two years
Intensive design and technical tuition for those intending to proceed to the practice of architecture.

Part Three. Practical. Two years
Working in an architect's office to gain practical experience. May be undertaken after diploma or "sandwiched" between components.

As in most areas of activity, computers have taken over many of the traditional skills, particularly technical drawing, as well as alleviating the drudgery of writing specifications , schedules or minutes of meetings, and computer-aided design skills now form part of the curriculum in schools.

Architecture is now one of the longest and most arduous courses available, and the knowledge and expertise of graduates are generally of a higher standard than previously.

But, as with most vocational subjects, it is difficult, if not impossible, to impart practical experience in an academic institution. Design is theoretical and students emerge with only about 50% of the skills required to practise, despite the "years out" when they may only be given menial tasks.

Practitioners continue to complain that students and graduates know little of the "real world". Academics counter that in a school of architecture it is more important to foster imagination and creativity.

However, emerging generations, brought up with information technology, tend to be visually more literate than previously, with a better understanding of environmental and design matters. This may help to break down the barriers of jargon that architects, like all professions, protect themselves with.

Architecture, like art, is still considered an inferior subject in schools and, until it is added to the curriculum, general ignorance of this vital aspect of life will persist.

is for Rome

In 300 years Rome grew from a country town to an imperial capital and mighty military power.

The **Romans** perfected the art of the take-over. First they took over the **Etruscans**, then they took over **Italy**, and finally they took over the whole world, or what they thought was the whole world: **Europe**, **Asia Minor** and **North Africa**.

Like movie moguls they took over **Greek** ideas (see *T is for Temples*) and inflated them into big vulgar productions for the benefit of the state. Colonising became conquering, administration became bureaucracy, and architecture became engineering. Where the Greek states imposed order locally, Roman imperialism steamrollered over whole countries, destroying cultures and imposing its rule by military might, technological superiority and... architecture.

The Romans imported their imperial, classical stone architecture, ignoring local tradition. Huge monuments such as **triumphal arches** were designed to overawe the natives.

The Greeks travelled chiefly by sea, in
harmony with nature. The Romans drove
roads straight as a die over the whole
empire crossing anything in their path
and laying waste the landscape on either
side to prevent ambush.

Roman architecture and engineering
symbolised the order imposed on
conquered peoples and the peace, the **Pax
Romana**, enforced on warring tribes.

Colonies were transformed into Roman
estates under governors, and milked for
their resources which went to fill the
coffers of the ruling class, while trade and
industry extended over the whole empire.

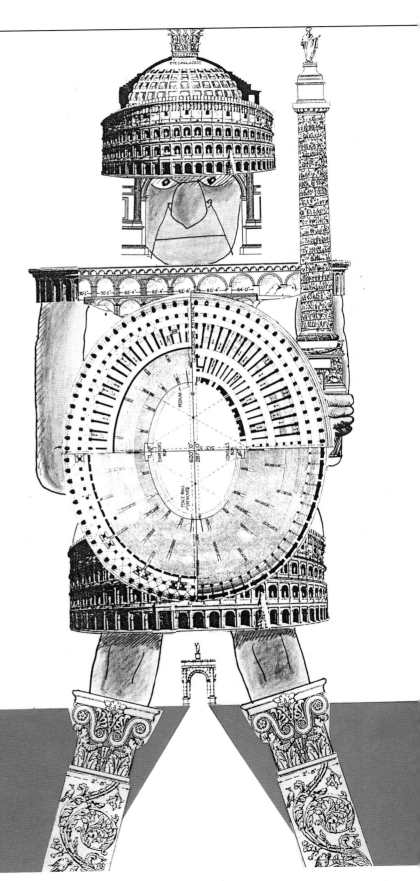

The world was one vast state with Rome at the centre. Each part supported and mirrored the whole.

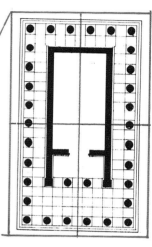

Buildings were equally directional in character, with emphatic fronts and closed-in sides and backs.

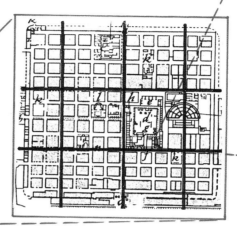

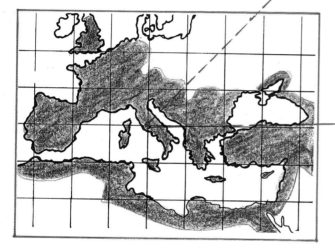

Each centralised and fortified city was laid out on a rectangular grid of streets based on military camp planning.

Roman cities were designed for their citizens, providing water supply, public baths, theatres, gymnasia, fountains and sports stadia, mostly financed by the rich under public pressure.

At the centre of the city was the **forum** for public meetings, shows or markets. It was not informal and open like the Greek agora, but enclosed and regular, with colonnades of shops, temples and a **basilica** (a kind of town hall/law court/ stock exchange), forming a protected inward-looking square.

Single-storey town houses for the well-to-do middle class were based on Greek models and consisted of two courtyards. The first, or **atrium (A)**, was entered from the street and was a public reception room, while the second, or **peristyle (P)**, was in the form of a private colonnaded garden with dining and other rooms leading from it.

The street frontage was occupied by shops which acted as a buffer against noise and burglary, and generally light was admitted through the open court. The houses were cool in summer but dark and cold in winter, lit by oil lamps and heated by smoky braziers. Underfloor central heating, developed for the public baths, was only used in houses in northern colonies and a piped water supply was not available except in the grandest houses. Interiors were highly decorated with mosaic floors, wall paintings and statues.

The majority of citizens and slaves (except those who had rooms in their owners' houses) lived in two small rooms in multi-storey tenements off the narrow, regimented streets.

Raised pavements protected pedestrians from the dirt and manure in the roads, which had stepping stone crossings.

The Romans created a vast empire although they were not exactly technical innovators. They adopted existing technology and reproduced it on a huge scale by organising human resources. The **arch** was one such element.

The Greeks knew of the arch but preferred the post and lintel which was limited by the length a single piece of stone could span.

An arch is made up of small pieces of stone or brick built around a wooden framework (centring), which is then removed.

An arch can therefore can be as big as you like. All that is required is the material and a few thousand slaves to build it!

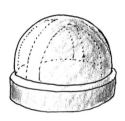

Arches can be combined to form continuous roofs (**barrel vaults**) or **domes** (see *X is for Xanadu*).

The pure arch tends to spread sideways which has to be countered by thick walls.

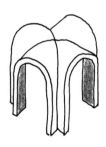

This problem was eventually solved by combining four inter-dependent arches known as a **groin vault**.

Arches of vast scale were exploited for massive engineering structures such as **viaducts** and **aqueducts** that carried military personnel, goods and water supplies across rivers and valleys all over the empire. Their strength was enhanced by the use of **concrete** for the main structure (see *M is for Modern*), which was then faced in brick or stone.

The arch system combined with concrete was applied to large public buildings such as baths, palaces and arenas, the biggest and best known of which is the **Colosseum in** Rome.

In these buildings different kinds of **classical orders** (see *T is for Temples*) are applied to the outside with little structural function, a departure from the Greeks who used only one order in a building as both structure and decoration.

The names of Roman engineer-architects are generally unknown, with the exception of **Vitruvius** who methodically set down rules for composing architecture using the three Greek orders plus two added by the Romans. These were the basis for rule books in the **Renaissance** and after (see *N is for Neo-Classica*l).

Ultimately the Roman Empire declined, principally as a result of its reliance on slaves and cheap labour rather than technology. The vast numbers of unpaid slaves were unable to participate as consumers of the empire's products and maintain its wealth.

While Rome perfected the take-over, **Christianity** developed the merger. As the Roman Empire disintegrated it was threatened from without by hordes of barbarian vandals, and from within by the Christians, a sect based on Jewish religion and Greek philosophy.

As the Empire disintegrated, Christianity grew stronger as people turned to mystical beliefs as a substitute for the certainties of the centralised state. In 330 the **Emperor Constantine** converted to the new religion, hoping to maintain his power.

But Christianity needed Rome – it had spread due to the Empire – and Rome needed Christianity in the face of the barbarian threat. A merger was arranged in which the Christians took over the old centralised Roman administration. Even slavery was maintained. "One God, one religion, one Church" replaced "one emperor, one ideal, one state." The Pope replicated the emperor as supreme leader.

In the West, Christians took over not the Romans' pagan temples, but their basilicas. These long halls with colonnades of pillars forming aisles on either side were ideal for the new religion which concentrated on congregational, community worship rather than secret rites.

Early Christian churches were derived from these basilicas, often incorporating columns quarried from abandoned Roman buildings. The rounded end where the Roman judge had sat became the **apse** in which the altar was located. The interior was decorated with Roman-style mosaics. Outside a bell tower or **campanile** called the faithful to worship.

Internally the emphasis of the early Christian church is horizontal, reflecting the Western notion of time as movement, change, progress and renewal.

In 330 Constantine moved his capital to **Byzantium** (renamed **Constantinople**), leaving the pope to hold the fort in Rome.

The move created an East-West schism in the Church which was made permanent in 800 and which is reflected in two different forms of architecture.

In 527 **Justinian** became emperor in the East and created a power base to rival Rome. It eventually extended to **Venice** and **Ravenna** in Italy, and was expressed in the building of the massive church of **Hagia Sophia**, **Constantinople**.

In the East, the **Byzantine** early Christian style adapted the centralised and domed Roman temple for churches. These also followed the Eastern tradition of brick structures (there was a lack of stone) and small windows to counteract the hot and dry climate. Congegations were accommodated but mystery and remoteness were a feature of the Eastern church ceremony, reinforced by the cosmic symbolism of the dome form. The development of the **pendentive**, derived from the groin vault, made it possible to sit a dome on a square and admit light from above.

Following Eastern tradition, the **Byzantine** church did not allow representational images and the interiors are decorated with mosaics in geometrical patterns.

Internally the emphasis of a Byzantine church is vertical and calm, reflecting the Eastern concept of time as unchanging, whole and eternal.

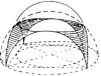

Having first merged with the old Roman Empire and then taken it over, the Christian Church did the same to the barbarians. **Charlemagne,** leader of the Franks, was appointed **Holy Roman Emperor** in 800.

Together, pope and emperor divided Europe into separate countries, each ruled by a combination of their agents, chieftans who had proclaimed themselves king and sworn to defend the faith, and bishops who had powerful positions at court.

As Church and barbarian united centrally and locally, so new ecclestiastical and (now) secular buildings combined Roman forms (arches, domes) with local constructional methods (brick, sloping roofs) which were adapted to indigenous climates. This is known as the **Romanesque** (**Norman** in Britain) style.

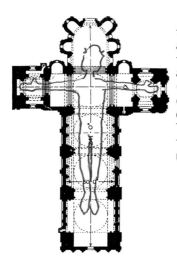

Monastic churches employed the Roman basilica model with added side altars conveniently forming a cross on plan, and an enlarged west end (following Eastern custom churches pointed towards the east) to accommodate the laity. The main body of the church, the nave, was occupied by the monks.

Instead of timber roofs, early Romanesque churches used a form of the Roman barrel vault which was more permanent and fireproof. Later, abbey church roofs combined the dome, arch and barrel vault to form the **ribbed vault** (see *G is for Gothic*) made up of two crossed arches with an in-filling of small stones, which eventually developed into the fan vault.

Nation-states were controlled by the Church and the monarchy, answerable to Rome but operating locally through the aristocracy and the clergy.

The Church maintained its power through the **monasteries**, self-sufficient communities of monks who needed no contact with the outside world. Monasteries were like small towns, containing every kind of facility from libraries to a prison and incorporating fields, mills, wine-making and stables.

The lord's castle, developed by the Normans, was an equally exclusive world. At its centre stood a tower (the **keep**), with living areas on several levels and protected from the hostile outside world by a high wall (the **bailey**).

S is for styles

The **Modern Movement** was in part a reaction against the style wars of the late 18th century when modern structures were "dressed up" in a variety of historical styles. The Modern Movement aimed to "return" to rational, fundamental principles inspired by the "true" structural expression found in Greek or Gothic buildings, as well as the new technology. There was also a social programme whereby architecture would serve the whole of society as opposed to a privileged class or elite.

But in the hands of mediocre architects, modernism became just another style, either narrowly orthogonal (rectilinear) or watered-down Le Corbusier (qv). In America the architect **Philip Johnson** even coined the term "**International Style**". It was a style that looked rational and scientific, having the repetitive, gridded appearance of graph paper, but was in reality no more functional or objective than any other architecture. The social programme was diluted and compromised by state or private agencies. Architects, it seemed, were more interested in style than content.

(Cartoon by Steinberg)

Following the end of the postwar hegemony of the orthogonal mode of modernism in the late 1970s, architecture, along with all the arts, dissolved into a plurality of directions. Architects rediscovered the many 20th-century alternatives to orthodox Functionalism that had been marginalised: Art Nouveau, Art Deco, Constructivism, Expressionism, organic, biomorphic and so on. A new battle of the styles emerged and, just as the Victorians had ignored the environmental problems resulting from the industrial revolution (see *I is for Industrial*), so late 20th-century architects shut their eyes to world problems of pollution, poverty and political repression as they served the new global capitalists.

From the 1950s there *was* an alternative to hard-line modernism based on vernacular (qv) or traditional local buildings but using modern technology: what might be termed **Pseudo-Vernacular**.

The style had its origins in Scandinavia and pre-war Expressionism, and in North European countries was characterised by the use of brick, tile and pitched (sloping) roofs. Confined to small buildings or houses it had some success, but when it was inflated to dress up large-scale bureaucratic blocks, high-rise housing or commercial developments with out-of-scale fake-folksy exteriors to pacify local planners, it tended to be ludicrous.

LOCAL GOVERNMENT BUREAUCRACY

SHOPPING CENTRE AND MULTI·STOREY CARPARK

HIGH-RISE WORKER'S HOUSING

The supposed real challenge to old modernism flowered in the 1980s as the short-lived **Post-Modern** movement whose theoretical basis originated in America in the late 1960s (see *U is for USA*).

Post-Modernism purported to return to the **language** of **sign** and **symbol** that its proponents saw as characterising historic architecture, as well as reverting to ornament, texture and colour. If modern architecture was alien and disliked, the argument went, the remedy was to include traditional (**popular**) elements. In practice, this often meant tacking bits of stripped classicism onto basically modern buildings in an **ironic** (jokey) way.

This attempt to graft traditional values onto modern concepts chimed well with the **Reagan/Thatcher** *laissez-faire* political philosophy of the 1980s. **London Docklands** developments where vast tracts of industrial land is given over to lumpen Post-Modern commercial developments were a prime example.

DOGLANDS...

In the search for 20th-century precedents as an alternative to modernism, even Neo-Classicism (qv) – or now rather **Post-Modern Classicism** was revived to be applied to office blocks, multistorey housing and even airport terminals.

Post-Modern Classicism was given a boost by **Prince Charles** when he assumed the role of critic of modern architecture in the mid-1980s, intervening in projects featuring modern designs with the result that they were replaced by Post-Modern Classical schemes. But Prince Charles' vision of a return to a mythical golden age of happy village communities was soon confined to the (classical) dustbin and the new modernists regained the initiative. But his intervention spawned a general debate and media awareness of architecture.

In Britain in the 1970s the Modern Movement revived, particularly in the **High-Tech** architecture of **Norman Foster** and **Richard Rogers**, now part of the beknighted establishment.

High-Tech follows the modernist principle of employing the most up-to-date technology available, and claims to have overcome the deficiencies of earlier steel and glass buildings by advances in the same technology.

For High-Tech architects, heavy masonry construction went out with the steam engine. Drawing on pioneers of lightweight structures like **Buckminster Fuller,** as well as aircraft technology, their forte is spacious, highly serviced "sheds" such as museums, factories, transport termini, corporate office HQs or multinational banks. Another influence is the **Futurist** and **Russian Constructivist** paper projects of 80 years ago (see *F is for Futurism*) where lifts and services were placed on the outside of buildings or roofs were suspended from masts to provide flexible and adaptable floor space. However, this facility is rarely used in practice and can result in external maintenance headaches.

Out of the decline of Post-Modernism emerged a late 20th-century version of modern architecture that might be termed **Mannerist Modern.**

Rather than the strictly homogenous character of Old Modern or the Toy Town silliness of Post-Modernism, Mannerist Modern features a mixture or collage of forms, materials and colours. **Rationalism** is crossed with **Vernacular**, **High-Tech** with **Organic**, early **Corbusier** with **Mies van der Rohe**, and so on. It may claim influences outside architecture, such as cinema, literature or fine art. At best, Mannerist Modern produces richer, more flexible buildings and can be adapted to update historic buildings; at worst it is over ostentatious and crassly self-publicising.

The major new style of the 1990s was **Deconstruction** which claimed a theoretical basis in French structuralist literary criticism and linguistic philosophy – a tenuous connection argued in obscure and arcane architectural texts.

The stylistic feature of Deconstruction is an aversion to the rectangle, the horizontal and the vertical. It aims to shock, jolt and disrupt by a collision or explosion of dynamic forms. In its linear version it derives from **Russian Constructivist** art and architecture (see *F is for Futurism*) and may invoke literary and topographical symbolism.

In freer, organic or Modern Baroque mode, such as the **Guggenheim Museum** in **Bilbao** – an example of the art gallery as colonial cultural temple – it relates to animal or plant forms. In both cases the (computer-generated) sculptural effects tend to be forced, metal sheeting bent round a steel armature (right), for example, and the exterior bearing little resemblance to the interior.

In lesser hands the style may have its dangers. We are physiologically designed to relate to horizontals and verticals, and when these go out of kilter we may feel ill or drunk.

T is for temples

A temple is a permanent building to house a deity, derived from the primitive shrine (see *A is for Architecture*), or a public place of worship.

During the **Bronze Age** in **Mesopotamia** in the Middle East, large temples raised up on ziggurats were not only shrines to the deity but residences and observatories for the ruling priest class who practised astrology as part of their polytheistic religion. The temples were also contained stores for the surplus food produced by forced labour in the fertile river valley and used to buy imported materials and support capital projects.

EVER GET THE FEELING YOU'RE BEING WATCHED?

Such large-scale projects involving mass slave labour required considerable organisation and planning.

In order to keep a tight check on materials, the priests developed methods of counting and writing.

The measurement in building was the cubit or forearm-length, but for large-scale building this was inadequate.

Thus a standard measure was devised using a wooden or metal rod marked off into units.

In Mesopotamia there were few trees and little usable stone and importing these materials was expensive. There was, however, plenty of one material – mud – for making sun-dried bricks and tiles to construct massive temple walls. The bricks and tiles were glazed in bright colours. Because of the dry hot climate, walls were pierced by small openings and formed cool inner courtyards protected from the sun.

Through laying square floor tiles and counting stacks of bricks, methods of calculating area and volume evolved.

The architects of the temples were, of course, the priests, who claimed they received the plans direct from the gods in their sleep.

The cruel militaristic and war-like **Assyrians** in the north, who took over cities such as Babylon, ruled from ostentatious temple/palace fortresses protected by sacred bulls.

The pyramids are famous as the timeless symbols of the static nature of **Ancient Egyptian** society, but the Egyptian temples made a significant contribution to architecture in the development of the internal colonnade composed of **column** and **lintel**.

The rulers of Egypt, the **Pharoahs**, were equally kings, high priests and gods in one person and exercised control over this world and the next. As in Mesopotamia, religion consisted of many triads of gods, headed by Osiris, the god of the dead, which symbolised nature and the climate of the fertile Nile valley on which the civilisation depended.

Only the Pharoahs and priests had access to the inner temples which were protected externally by thick, sloping walls on which were recorded historical events. The entrance was often marked by **pylons** and the approach lined with **sphinxes**.

The priests conducted their secret rites among colonnades of columns which were formed of quarried stone (sandstone and limestone) shaped by stone tools.

The columns had decorated tops (capitals) in the form of stylised lotus buds, palms or papyrus flowers which, like the gods, were symbols of the abundance and fertility of the Nile.
The stylised arrangement of column bases, fluted shafts and flower-like capitals probably evolved from primitive buildings constructed of unmodified organic materials such as bundles of reeds with their heads left on and tied together to form posts.

In **Ancient Greece** the evolution of the temple reached perfection as the **classical** stone colonnaded building, a system of proportion and detail that has dominated architecture ever since. Like so much else of our culture, the Greeks virtually invented architecture.

Iron Age technology made tools and weapons generally available and spelt the destruction of the old autocratic rulers who depended on the exclusivity of Bronze Age implements. In Greece a middle class of merchants, financiers and farmer-landowners emerged to organise society according to their needs as property-owning, free-thinking individuals. Culture, religion and architecture were adapted to these needs.

Religion no longer glorified a ruling priest class, but was personalised. The pantheon of gods was like a family of superhumans.

Art was no longer in the sole service of power and religion, but now developed to celebrate individual human beings.

Science and philosophy no longer served the practical requirements of a ruler, but sought to question the natural world objectively.

The centre of city-states such as **Athens** was the **agora**, where political, commercial and cultural activities took place. It comprised a market square and colonnades (outdoor activity was appropriate to the warm, temperate climate), council chamber, theatre and gymnasium. Athens pioneered a form of democracy: everyone had a vote as long as they were white, male and owned property. Temples were located nearby, raised up on an **acropolis** or citadel.

Although religion did not dominate as it did in Egypt, the temples have survived as pale ruins to typify Greek civilisation rather than the agorae (or spaces between buildings) where a form of democracy was developed.

The Greek temples developed from primitive shrines built of timber, to be transmuted and conventionalised in stone in various styles or **orders** – canonic (standard) forms that were refined and perfected over generations. Columns formed the external structure supporting the roof and the **pediments** (gable ends).

There were **three** Greek orders, each with its own character that was applied to the appropriate type and size of building:

DORIC
Symbolic of masculine power. The column form probably derived from tooling marks on wooden posts.

IONIC
Symbolic of female grace and slenderness. The capital was based on natural or organic forms like shells or ram's horns.

CORINTHIAN
Tree or plant-like, similar to Egyptian columns. The capital is a stylised version of **acanthus** leaves growing round a pot.

The Parthenon in Athens, temple to the goddess Athena, and the apotheosis
of the Doric order, was built on the Acropolis by the statesman Pericles,
head of the Populist Party, to celebrate victory over the Persian invaders.

Greek temples were not designed for
congregational worship or as seats
of power, but were shrines for statues
with spaces in front for sacrifices or
ceremonies.

They were as much large pieces
of sculpture as buildings and their
designers were equally sculptors,
builders and architects.

Such temples were not built from pre-
formed finished parts but put up in a
rough stone form to be finished by teams
of masons. Sculptors filled in the **pedimen**
(A) and **frieze** (B) with narratives of
famous victories. The whole building was
painted in multicolours like the Gothic
cathedrals (*see G is for Gothic*) in the
Middle Ages.

Early Greek sculptures had been as stiff and stylised as Egyptian ones, but sculptors discovered
that by distorting proportions and emphasising features, an impression of life and movement
could be expressed.

The Parthenon, too, is given "life" by distortion of its parts. It appears to be geometrically
perfect, with true horizontals and verticals, but this is achieved by the optical illusion of
slightly curving lines to make the building "sing".

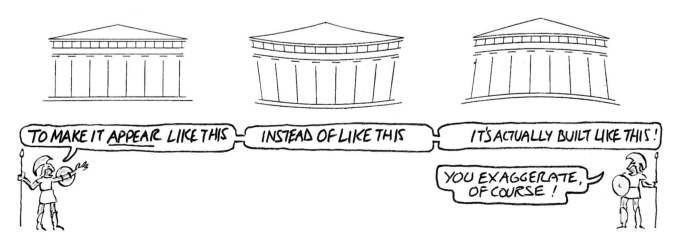

This unity of architecture and sculpture is well demonstrated in another temple on the Acropolis, the **Erechtheion**, where **Caryatids** – statues of women – hold up the porch roof.

The temples on the Acropolis in Athens ( ), and the Agora itself (B), although individually **symmetrical** (presenting a mirror image each side of a centre line) are sited informally (**asymmetrically**), possibly in relation to religious processional routes (C). The areas in between constitute a naturally inspired enclosed sacred space (**temenos**). In this way the classical temples on the Acropolis relate to their natural surroundings and, from inside the colonnades, frame the landscape.

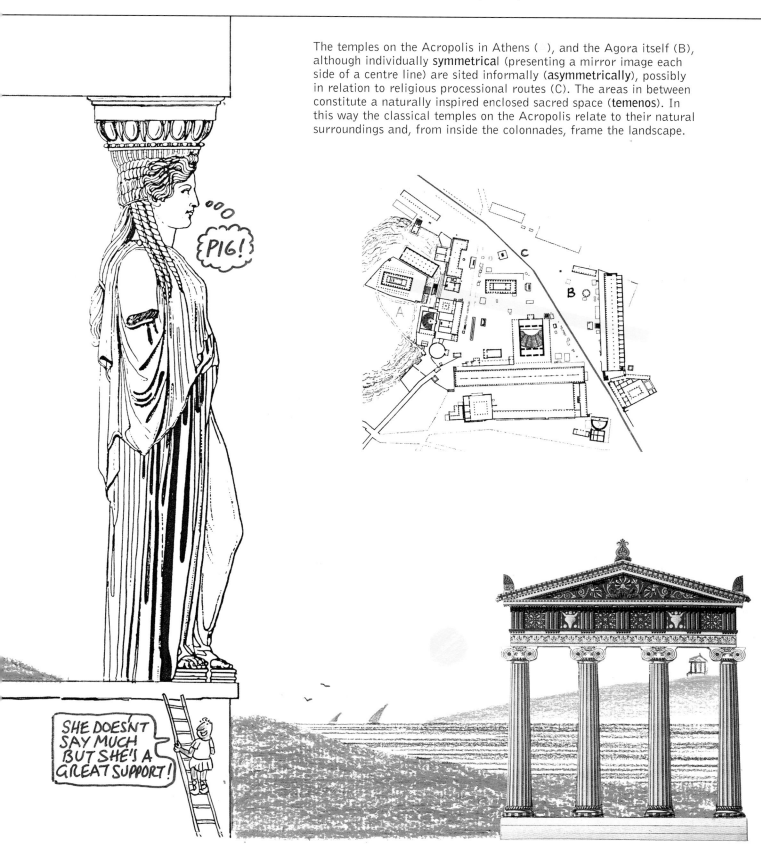

PIG!

SHE DOESN'T SAY MUCH BUT SHE'S A GREAT SUPPORT!

The nature of Christianity required congregational churches rather than temples to the deity, as did the other great religion, **Islam**, while **Hindus** and **Buddhists** worshipped at shrines.

Islam means literally "surrender" to the will of God (**Allah**) as interpreted in the **Koran**, the sacred book of the word of God dictated to the prophet **Muhammed**.

From its foundation in 7th-century Arabia, Islam spread rapidly through a combination of religious fervour and military colonialism. Within three centuries it reached the Middle East, the north coast of Africa and southern Spain.

The **mosque** (literally a place for prostration), provides communal prayer five times a day, but it also has a political function appropriate to a state religion, and may include a law court, school and hospital. According to the Koran, Allah has no form and altars and figurative images are forbidden. Mosques are renowned for their highly coloured geometric decoration inside and out.

Early mosques consisted of a large court with a central fountain for ablutions, surrounded by colonnades and with a larger end containing a pulpit and facing towards **Mecca**, the birthplace of **Muhammed**. The faithful were called to prayer from the top of slender towers, or **minarets**.

Islamic architecture is also characterised by the variety of its arch forms.

POINTED

OGEE

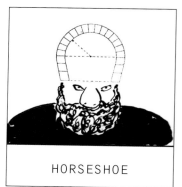

HORSESHOE

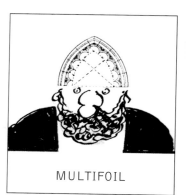

MULTIFOIL

After the fall of Constantinople in 1453, Islam was dominated by the Turkish **Ottoman Empire** which developed large monumental domed mosques, in stone or brick, modelled on **Hagia Sophia** in Istanbul (see *R is for Rome*).

The most famous Islamic building is, of course, the **Taj Mahal** in **Agra, India**, a mausoleum based on mosque elements with dome, flat decorated screens and minarets. It was built by the all-powerful ruler **Shah Jahan** for his young wife who died in childbirth, and is exceptional for its integration of pools and landscaping.

Islam spread to India from the northwest, culminating in the **Mogul Empire**'s takeover of the capital Delhi in 1193 in conflict with the existing **Buddhist**, **Hindu** and **Jain** traditions.

Buddha (the Enlightened One) was born in India in 563 and Buddhism represented a breakaway from the power of the Brahmin priesthood and rigid caste system.

In contrast to the monotheistic, communal Islam, Buddhism and Hinduism are relatively private, self-orientated and peace-centred religions involving transcendental meditation and the spiritual journey to attain enlightenment. The Hindu temple is itself an object of worship as a shrine to one or more of a large pantheon of gods and typically is covered in stone carvings and statues representing the journey from the temporal to the spiritual world, and including a celebration of fertility and eroticism. Temples may be hewn out of rock or be in the form of **stupas**, conical mounds that symbolise the universe.

IT'S HEAVEN UP HERE !

IT'S PRETTY GOOD DOWN HERE TOO!

is for USA

The **Industrial Revolution** arrived late in the United States in the mid-19th century, but rapidly transformed the country which developed on a vast scale unencumbered by social or industrial traditions. Within 20 years the USA changed from a rural economy based on small-scale farming and slavery to an urban industrial one. The railways and coal, iron and steel production, coupled with unfettered private enterprise, transformed the country. By the end of the century, the machine, mass production and big business had made America the richest state in the world.

But wealth and power lay in the hands of a small group of multimillionaires and price-fixing companies and trusts.

Capitalists like **Rockefeller** (oil) and **Vanderbilt** (railways) exercised influence over presidents and governments through power and wealth. They were like self-made kings and the ostentatious private mansions they built were appropriately in the French absolute monarch's Baroque style.

Industrial America was built on mass production, cheap immigrant labour and ruthless
financial dealing. In contrast to Europe, materials were plentiful and skilled labour scarce.
Mass-produced goods were accepted and mass production, not just of new materials like
cement and steel, but also brick, stone and especially timber, was the norm.

IVE ME YOUR TIRED.... YOUR POOR... YOUR HUDDLED MASSES OF CHEAP LABOR...

Factory-produced timber and cheap nails and screws gave rise to "**balloon frame**" structures
(so called because of their lightness). Standard wooden sections were simply nailed together
and stiffened by external matchboarding, doing away with the traditional carpentry joints.
Here also the machine made up for lack of craftsmen. Buildings built like this were light, easy
to prefabricate and transport, ideal for the setting up of new frontier towns in the expansion
of the west.

But while the Industrial Revolution in the USA made cheap housing available, it transformed the buildings of industry and big business.

As cities grew at a fast rate, downtown land increased in cost and the vast administrative centres required to run the enterprises started to expand upwards into "skyscraper" office blocks.

Without the inventions of the Industrial Revolution skyscrapers would not have been possible. Rolled-steel columns and beams, lifts and revolving doors, central heating, electric light, water closets and modern plumbing, and the telephone all enabled buildings to be multistorey. Not to mention the huge profits that financed them.

The needs of big business and the newly-available technology enabled architects to design skyscrapers, but what were they to look like? There was no historic precedent for such tall multifloored buildings.

In the first phase of skyscrapers in 1890s **Chicago**, capital of the Midwest and less under European influence – the style was functional and utilitarian. The investment banker patrons wanted the most economic, no-frills solutions and the grid of the steel structures, clad in stone or tile, was expressed on the outside. Minimal classical-based ornament was confined to key points on the grid and this, combined with long windows split into three parts, became known as the **Chicago Style**.

The second, or **eclectic,** phase of skyscraper building took place mainly in **New York.** Here where there were more resources and confidence, the historic styles were applied to these soaring structures, accommodating the complex stepping-back required by the city planners' daylight regulations.

The skeleton frames were clad in adopted versions of historic architecture: a gigantic classical column complete with base and capital, a Gothic cathedral stretched out like toffee, several Renaissance palaces on top of each other, a gigantic Baroque castle... the variations were endless as architects and their big-business clients vied with each other to go ever higher and be ever more ostentatious.

During the 1920s and 1930s and through the **Depression,** the move to the cities increased. The middle classes settled in suburbs and the mass-produced car, pioneered by **Henry Ford,** started to take over as the main form of transport.

In New York the **Rockefeller Center** and the **Empire State Building** reached staggering heights and both had public elements, the former containing **Radio City.** The 1930s ushered in the age of the entertainment industry: radio, movies, records, jazz and musical shows. For a time a third style flourished: **Art Moderne** or **Art Deco**, the Jazz Age Baroque and a different dress for skyscrapers such as the **Chrysler** building for the now massive car industry. The origins of Art Deco are diverse. Its eclectic decorative style was a mixture of Red Indian symbolism, Cubism, Futurism, Expressionism and neo-Egyptian, often applied to buildings in the form of coloured terracotta or glazed ceramic tiles. In the 1940s and 1950s the vast **movie palaces** in the USA and Europe continued to exploit the style to the full, but the Second World War and the Functionalists put an end to its use for other buildings.

RUINED!

The fourth phase of skyscraper building, in the **Modern Movement** or **Functionalist** style, flowered after the Second World War, reverting to the austere principles of the Chicago Style.

Functionalism was imported from Europe by pioneer modern architects who had fled Nazi Germany to practise in the land of high capitalism.

Now a new liason flourished between the powerful postwar corporations, particularly those selling consumer products, and the new technology.

Deploring the "decadence" of Art Deco ornamentation, the architects designed the urban headquarters of consumer capitalism in the reductive, abstract, gridded style of the Modern Movement.

Now there were no defined tops or bases to the skyscrapers, merely an arbitrary cutting off of the grid at the flat roof, symbolising perhaps fluctuations in stock market-led profits.

At the end of the 1970s there was a reaction to the hegemony and "elitist" austerity of Functionalism in the form of **Post-Modernism,** which had developed in the USA (see overleaf and *S is for Styles*).

Just as the Functionalists had looked to Chicago, Post-Modern skyscrapers took up the New York "wedding cake" style, but in a drastically simplified form. Towers were designed with tops like Regency cabinets, Gothic horror movie castles or French Baroque palaces.

Even Art Deco was revived as the dustbin of history was scavenged in the attempt to dress up the new temples of capitalism in a populist style.

With the end of Post-Modernism, skyscrapers now adopt a generally High-Tech approach but using more "interesting" silhouettes which might be based on organic form.

American modern architects like **Robert Venturi** were among the first to propound an alternative to hard-line "alien" modernism in the early 1970s.

Following **Pop Art's** celebration of "unconscious" art in advertising or comics, Venturi sought inspiration for a **popular** modern architecture in areas where commercial enterprise had created buildings and environments free from the intervention of architects and planners.

Las Vegas, the entertainment city in **Nevada**, for example, is a sprawling eclectic jumble of styles from modernist to pseudo-Roman. Buildings are little more than sheds with signs and displays to attract customers off the road and into the gambling casinos.

DISORDER IS AN ORDER WE CANNOT SEE !

At night a totally different environment is revealed, hidden by day, and formed by the electric illuminations: space is defined not by buildings, but by artificial light.

By analysing the apparent chaos of Las Vegas, Venturi attempted to evolve a self-conscious design philosophy for an "ordinary" and "inclusive" popular modern architecture of decorated sheds with obvious "fronts and backs" that employed traditional signs and imagery.
The approach opened the Pandora's box of **Post-Modernism** and a return to pastiche and art-for-art's-sake historicism. Far from being popular it represented more arcane games by architects for architects.

Venturi conveniently ignored the political and social aspects of Vegas – a gangster community which exploits women, prostitution, drug-pushing and greed, and pollutes its desert location.

 # is for vernacular

In spite of their life of drudgery (or because of it) workers and peasants the world over evolved their own folk counter-cultures, crafts, costumes, dances and ballads.

This alternative **vernacular** culture was also expressed in buildings. For centuries homes were built by their inhabitants, or by local builders. They catered for specific needs using resources that were to hand, ancient traditional techniques and simple tools.

The form of dwellings was affected by the natural environment and materials available (see *B is for Building*) as well as cultural traditions, whether these were nomadic with portable houses (see *Y is for Yurt*) or static with homes hewn from rock. In northern climes the process of building might be as follows:

Ideally the site for building would be close to a stream and good pasture, sheltered from the wind and high enough to avoid flooding.

There might be brick kilns nearby so that bricks could be brought to site by oxen. Bricks were rare and expensive and used sparingly.

A fire would be needed for warmth and cooking. Bricks would be ideal for the construction of a chimney and fireplace and to add stability.

The structure would be formed from roughly hewn curved trees or branches fixed together like wish bones and embedded in the ground.

Dried straw or reeds would be tied in bundles and fastened in layers over a basket-weave of straight sticks to form a **thatched roof.**

The walls were made of mud and sticks. First a basketweave of sticks (**wattle**) was built as a base to be plastered over with mud (**daub**).

Windows were kept to a minimum, especially on north-facing walls. Ill-fitting shutters and doors kept some heat in but cut out daylight.

An iron window with glass fixed in a lead framework, made by the local smith, was such an expensive possession it would be taken by the owners when they moved.

The finished house could be strong and weathertight but even in this idealised version, was usually damp, draughty and smoke-filled.

But the simple, functional cottage represented a oneness with its natural surroundings. From their home, the peasant family could see the source of all their building materials: timber from the forest, clay from the earth for the bricks and walls, reeds from the river and straw for the thatched roof. Thousands of such dwellings were built all over Europe during the agrarian era.

Vernacular building was ignored by the aesthetic elites, and certainly not thought of as architecture, until the 18th-century romantic and patronising cult of the **picturesque** and the primitive. **Mary Antoinette**, the Queen of France, even played out her rural fantasies by dressing up as a milkmaid.

But its impact on mainstream architecture was brought to bear in the mid-19th century by two British critics of the Industrial Revolution, **William Morris** and **John Ruskin**. Ruskin and Morris had both been influenced by Pugin and the Gothic Revival (see *G is for Gothic*) and **Rousseau**'s romantic notion of primitive man, born free but everywhere in chains, as well as by new ideas regarding the role of the artist which developed after the second French revolution of 1848. Revolutionary artists demanded an art in the service of the people, by the people and for the people, and supported the revolution against the privileged elite who had previously been their patrons.

For Morris and Ruskin, classical architecture was both foreign and the imposition of ruling-class taste on society. Horrified by the effects of the Industrial Revolution, they looked back to the **Middle Ages** when they believed workers had pride in their craft and were not slaves to the machines of capitalism.

Morris went further. He proclaimed that if art, design and architecture were as important as cultured people said they were, they should be accessible to everybody and not merely the elite. He wanted architects to turn their attentions away from historic styling and tackle the terrible inhuman environment created by industrialisation. These ideas gave rise to the **Arts and Crafts** movement which drew inspiration from pre-classical Nordic and medieval culture.

Morris was not against the machine as such, as long as it was used for the benefit of society and not to enslave and alienate the workforce.

Morris believed that an architecture for the people should draw inspiration not from classical Italian palazzi, but from the simple houses and churches of rural England. In his view these were as worthy of the name 'architecture' as the grand monuments.

I HAVE HOPE THAT IT WILL BE FROM SUCH NECESSARY, UNPRETENTIOUS BUILDINGS THAT THE NEW AND GENUINE ARCHITECTURE WILL SPRING, RATHER THAN EXPERIMENTS IN CONSCIOUS STYLE...
(Morris)

For Morris, vernacular architecture was honest, truly British, appropriate to the climate and built of natural, local untreated materials in contrast to the imported marble and hardwoods used in classical boxes.

The **Red House** of 1859, near London, was designed for Morris and his circle of **Pre-Raphaelite** friends by the young architect **Philip Webb** to express their ideas about a new, free architecture inspired by native vernacular building.

Today the Red House looks like a slightly austere, typically Victorian house, but when it was completed it caused a sensation. It was thought shocking that "cultured" people should attempt to ape the "crude" buildings of the lower classes. The **English Free Architecture** movement that it spawned had a great influence on the development of modern architecture.

The Red House was an expression of all Morris' influences and aims at the time:

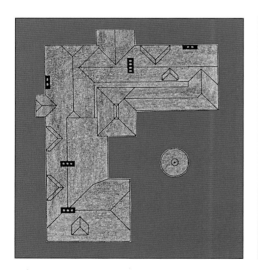

RATIONALISM	NATIONALISM	ROMANTICISM
Instead of starting with a symmetrical front and fitting the rooms in behind, which was the classical method, the Red House was designed from the inside out. Each room was considered in terms of its light and view, with artists' studios facing north, and arranged asymmetrically round the garden.	The materials were not imported but were local red brick and tile. Internally timber was left natural and untreated. Like vernacular buildings the house mixed diverse elements – turrets, Gothic pointed arches, Georgian sash windows, circular Medieval windows and so on – in an **eclectic** manner.	Instead of cutting all the trees down to make a flat table on which to place the house, which then was generally the norm, the house was built amidst the trees on an orchard site in a natural and "rustic" manner. The well is a symbol of this unity of house and nature, as are the untreated materials.

The Red House celebrated the essence of domesticity, with steep protective roofs, tall chimneys, inviting entrance porch, warm materials and "natural" garden. It set the style for British houses from then on (see *H is for Housing*).

Morris' view of the noble worker was patronising and romanticised, and his moralising zeal for improving the lot of the lower orders was typical of the Victorian era. Real workers were too busy organising unions to worry about a return to joyful labour and Morris realised that his radical ideas about art and craft could not happen without a social and political change.

But the Arts and Crafts style was a success with the affluent middle class, who adopted the new architecture in the new suburbs. It enabled the stockbroker and banker to have the best of both worlds: the simple country life and a quick rail link to their city offices. (See *H is for Housing*).

The Arts and Crafts movement spread throughout northern Europe to **Germany**, **Austria**, **Belgium**, **Scotland**, **Denmark**, **Holland** and **Finland**. Each country adopted its own vernacular as an expression of nationalism in opposition to the Neo-Classical styles...

The Arts and Crafts house was so popular it has influenced suburban house building up to the present day, particularly in England, with tits semidetached and volume versions created by speculative builders.

If even the Arts and Crafts houses did not follow strict vernacular principles (building white stuccoed dwellings in areas where slate was the local material, for example), the postwar builder's house is a mass-produced, factory-made, land-guzzling, consumer product and nothing to do with local vernacular traditions. It may use plastic windows, cement "slates", and concrete bricks with mock "Tudorbethan" details stuck on. It provides an image of traditional domesticity which appeals to the consumer and mortgage lender alike.

...of the old regimes and empires or purely to celebrate new national consciousness The English Arts and Crafts movement influenced **American** architects like **Frank Lloyd Wright** (*see O is for Organic*) who, paradoxically, sought to break from European Neo-Classical influence.

The Arts and Crafts and **English Free Architecture** principles of simple, undecorated vernacular-based architecture influenced early Modern Movement architects (see *I is for Industrial*), although the former would have been horrified by the idea.

If the simplicity of the Arts and Crafts movement, and its successor Art Nouveau, helped create the functional style, it also fuelled the romantic **Expressionist** and **Organic** alternatives which were suppressed by the hard-line modernists in the 1930s.

After the Second World War, a Pseudo-Vernacular (see *S is for Styles*) or **International Vernacular** style emerged to be applied to large-scale buildings and characterised by the use of pitched roofs, brick and tiles and timber windows. Like International Modernism, it had little to do with local vernaculars and was usually most successful in non-urban settings. More suitable for a city context was the influence of the **Industrial Vernacular** – the mills, warehouses and factories of the Industrial Revolution which drew on local brickbuilding traditions adapted to larger constructions.

A GERMAN FARM

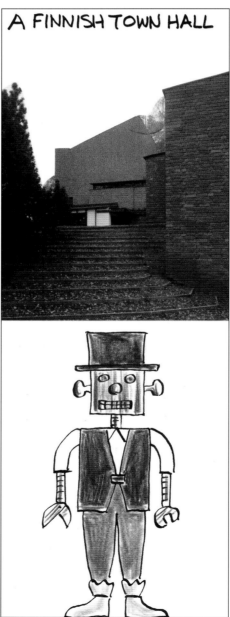

A FINNISH TOWN HALL

AN ENGLISH UNIVERSITY

Recently the use of simple technology which characterises the best vernacular building
has provided lessons for a sustainable, energy-efficient architecture (see *E is for Ecology*).

The forms of vernacular buildings have often evolved in response to particular
climatic conditions, and an energy-conscious contemporary architecture may draw
inspiration from oast house roofs, industrial chimneys or even animal structures
such as termite nests. The technology employed may vary from High Tech to timber,
grass roofs or straw.

As in good vernacular building, style is subjugated to energy-saving considerations.
Form follows environment.

⋈ is for women

The cartoon image of the architect in this book – white, male, middle-class, bearded and bow-tied – is a comic stereotype. Like all stereotypes it contains a half truth. All sorts of people are architects but the profession is still male-dominated.

More women study architecture now (some 34% of architectural students in Britain are female) but the drop-out rate is high. Only 12% of practising architects are women although they represent half the population. Very few are principals and where there is a man/woman partnership the man invariably gets the credit. Only 12% of architects are from minority ethnic backgrounds. There is more discrimination in architecture than other professions and part-time working and maternity leave are exceptions.

Because men dominate in architecture and town planning, environments tend to be designed in their own image. Priority is given to cars and roads while public transport is down-graded. Pedestrian safety tends to be overlooked with underpasses, narrow passages between buildings and cul-de-sacs which are frightening and potentially dangerous to most users, but especially women, children and elderly people. Family facilities such as crèches are rare, public toilet provision is unequal and access is often difficult. House design tends to be aimed at a middle-class model where the wife stays at home, confined to an isolated kitchen separate from the rest of the home.

If architecture and the built environment is not designed with women in mind, it may also disadvantage other groups of people.

The trouble is that architects and designers tend to design according to abstract aesthetic principles rather than considering the needs of people. The fictitious "standard" person (the "ergonome") depicted in design guides represents the average able-bodied male (around 20% of the population), and it is his needs that are catered for while all other people are excluded. These may include women, pregnant women, children, people pushing buggies, elderly people, culturally diverse people, short or tall people, people with poor eyesight or hearing, less than able-bodied people, people carrying loads, people with temporary injuries, people with physical disabilities (mobility, sight, hearing), people with psychological problems, and so on.

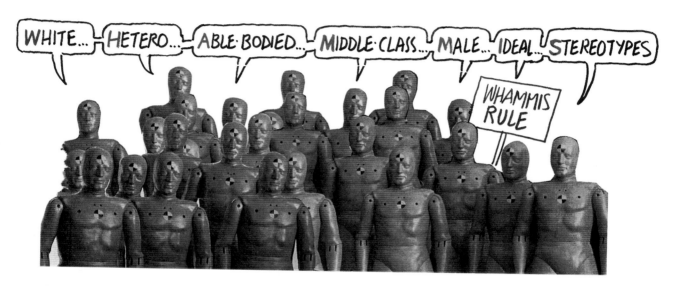

While most people can somehow adapt to bad design, the person confined to a wheelchair cannot overcome architectural barriers — steps, narrow toilets and doors or changes of level — to their right to access to the environment.

Legislation therefore concentrates on the wheelchair and this often leads to "special" provision such as ramps or side entrances which reinforce the disabled person's feeling of separateness.

Historically, monumental buildings were deliberately designed to exclude and be inaccessible, raised up on podia or flights of steps, symbolic of power and apartness.

The Modern Movement originally claimed to serve the whole population rather than the old elites but it singularly failed to develop a true democratic architecture. Buildings still made play with arbitrary changes of level, were raised up on steps for no good reason or perpetuated old design conventions. Scientific advances in technology were exploited but not the social sciences which studied people, anthropometrics and the psychology of space and colour. Style won over content.

ANCIENT...

AND MODERN

But today Information Technology and advances in materials technology make possible both public buildings and private houses which *are* accessible to everybody, comfortable and safe: **Universal Design**. Steps can be eliminated, colours and lighting designed for comfort rather than aesthetic whim, handles, taps and buttons easily operable even by those with physical or psychological difficulties and spacious lifts can be provided. Eventually doors, windows, lighting, security and most elements in the home will be operated by remote control devices which are currently the norm for electronic goods.

"GOD, I CANT STAND THIS PLACE ANYMORE..."

" AH, THAT'S BETTER ! "

is for Xanadu

In Xanadu did Kubla Khan,
A stately pleasure-dome decree:
(Samuel Taylor Coleridge)

In the 13th century the **Mongol** chieftan, **Kublai Khan**, son of Genghis, ruled a vast empire from the Volga to the Pacific and from Siberia to Iran. His power base was in **Beijing** and "Xanadu" was his summer palace on the Chinese border. Since there is no record of what this looked like we can, like Coleridge, invent it.

The dome, a form developed in the East, symbolises the head or cranium. Structurally it consists of a combination of crossing arches in compression and, like the arch, (see *R is for Rome*) is unlimited in size. Since the 19th century, domes have been formed from light or thin materials such as steel or reinforced concrete, but the principle remains the same.

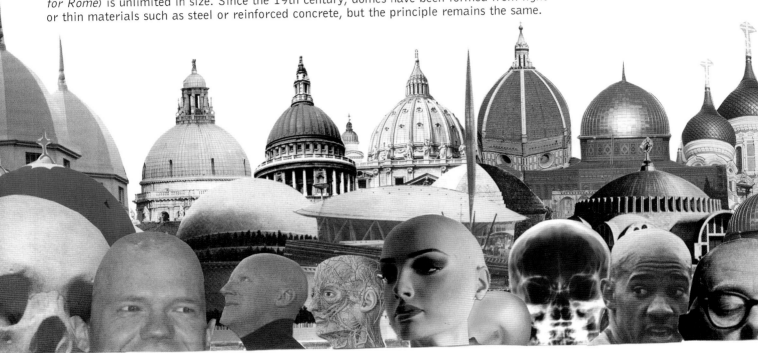

The controversial **Millennium Dome** in London is not a dome at all in the compression structural sense, but a tensile structure similar in principle to a tent. The "dome" is a plastic sheet (the canvas) suspended from steel masts (tent poles) by cables (guy ropes).

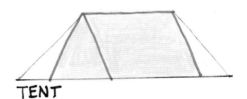

TENT

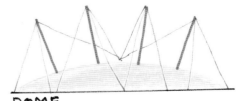

DOME

 is for yurt

The **yurt** is a tent-like portable dwelling used by nomadic peoples in north and central Asia, and consists of felt or skins stretched over a framework. Yurts provide shelter in extremes of temperature from hot to cold, and their aerodynamic form copes with severe winds. Yurts vary in character and those in **Mongolia** differ from shelters in **Kazakstan** and **Uzbekistan**.

The kit of parts usually consists of...

willow or poplar struts...

a roof wheel...

trellis...

felt...

girths and rope.

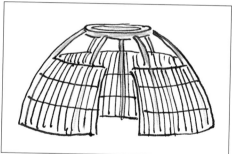

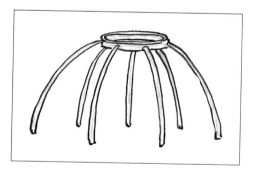

The floor of the yurt is formed by layers of felt placed onto the earth. This is covered by decorated rugs. The entrance door faces south for spiritual reasons and the place of honour for the head of the family is directly opposite.

The right side is the women's domain and sleeping area. The left side is for saddles and weapons as well as food storage. In the centre is the fire or stove for cooking and heating.

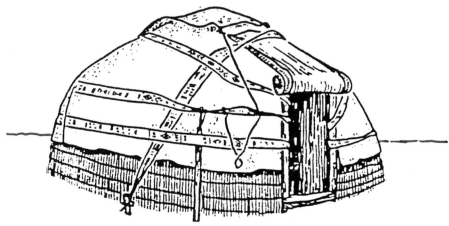

I'M WORRIED ABOUT MINE, HE KEEPS TALKING ABOUT "SETTLING DOWN"!

In the West the tent was modified where the principle of portable dwellings was required...
from the small military tent to the circus big top. Post-industrialisation, mobile homes
included the caravan and the Portacabin.

Since the 1970s tribal rock concert spectacles, previously dependent on inappropriate sports
stadia, have developed massive high-tech demountable stages and stage sets, made possible
by powerful portable lighting and PA systems which can be rapidly erected and taken down.
In one case the **Rolling Stones** played 33 cities in the USA in 15 weeks using the same
portable stage construction, including giant inflatable figures.

is for zoo

"...the city is not a concrete jungle, it is a human zoo."   Desmond Morris, *The Human Zoo*

The word "zoo" is an abbreviation of **zoological gardens** where wild animals are kept in captivity for the purposes of scientific study and public entertainment. In **England** the **Zoological Society**, inspired by the Jardin des Plantes in Paris, set up the **London Zoo** in 1828 with a layout designed by the architect **Decimus Burton**.
As the zoo developed in the 19th century, new kinds of animal enclosures requiring innovative building forms were added such as an aquarium, reptile house and insect house.

In the 20th century the London Zoo provided an opportunity for experimental modern architecture.

The Penguin Pool built in 1934 featured stunning concrete technology in its intertwining curved ramps.

Unfortunately it is not quite so successful in animal and human terms since the penguin's natural habitat is ice, shale and deep water, not shallow concrete pools, and the enclosing wall is too high for young children to see over.

The Aviary, built in 1962, is also advanced structurally, a kind of high-tech bird cage, into which viewers are introduced.

But it is restricting as a place to keep and view birdlife and is negotiated by a fairly narrow bridge, treacherous for families with young children.

The Elephant and Rhino House, built in 1965, is a brutalist concrete structure in the fashion of the time, a sort of parody of elephantine form. But it is far too small and limited for animals who normally roam in herds of up to 50.

Is there a parallel in these procrustean animal enclosures and Modern Movement architecture for people? Is there a further parallel in the current reaction against such treatment of animals in favour of "natural zoos" (which have been around since the 1930s), which have open parkland rather than cages or enclosures?

Finally we must not forget **the client**, without whom there would be no architecture and no book...

Index

Some of the illustrations in this book are based on cartoons which first appeared in *The Architects' Journal, Architectural Review, Building Design, Design Week* and *Built Environment*. Other material is based on parts of *Architecture for Beginners* (Louis Hellman, 1986).

92 Metro station, Paris 1900, by Hector Guimard (1867–1942); Casa Batlló, Barcelona, 1907, by Antonio Gaudí.

95 The Robie House, Chicago 1908, and Falling Water, Bear Run, Pennsylvania 1937–9, by Frank Lloyd Wright (1867–1959).

96 Johnson Wax Factory, Racine, Wisconsin 1936–9, by Frank Lloyd Wright.

97 Guggenheim Museum, New York 1942–60, by Frank Lloyd Wright.

98 Buildings by Santiago Calatrava, Jørn Utzon, Pier Luigi Nervi , Felix Candela, Bruce Goff, Foster Associates, Bart Simpson, etc.

100 The pyramids, Gizah BC3733–3566; St Peter's, Rome 1506–1626; the Colosseum, Rome AD 70–80; cathedral of Notre Dame, Paris 1163–c 97); Uffizi Palace, Florence 1560–?.

101 Cartoon by Osbert Lancaster (1908–86) from *Pillar to Post* (1938).

106 United Nations headquarters, New York 1950, by Le Corbusier, Wallace Harrison (1895–1981) and Max Abramovitz (1908–-). etc

108 Hong Kong and Shanghai Bank, Hong Kong 1984, by Norman Foster (1935–).

113 Tubular steel armchair 1926, by Marcel Breuer (1902–81). The Bauhaus, Dessau 1926, by Walter Gropius. Paintings by George Grosz (1893–1959).

116 Forum of Augustus, Rome AD 14; arch of Septimus Severus, Rome AD 204.

117 The Colosseum, Rome AD 70–80; Trajan's Column, Rome AD 112; Pont du Gard, Nimes 1st century AD.

118 Temple of Mars Ultor, Rome AD 14.

119 The House of the Tragic Poet, Pompeii; Street in Pompeii.

120 Pont du Gard, Nimes 1st century AD.

121 The Colosseum, Rome AD 70–80.

122 Santa Sabina, Rome 422–32.

123 Hagia Sophia, Constantinople 532–37.

124 The Campanile, Pisa 1174.

125 St Etienne, Caen 1068; Tower of London 1078.

126 Cartoon by Saul Steinberg.

128 Hillingdon Civic Centre, London 1976, by Robert Matthew Johnson Marshall; Ealing Town Centre, London 1985, by The Building Design Partnership; Byker Housing, Newcastle 1968–80, by Ralph Erskine.

130 Richmond Town Centre 1987, by Quinlan Terry (1937–).

131 Lloyds Building, London 1984, by Richard Rogers (1933–); Institute du Monde l'Arabe, Paris 1987, by Jean Nouvel (1945–); office block, Ipswich 1974, and Commerz Bank, Frankfurt 1997, by Norman Foster; Eden Project, Cornwall 2000, by Nicholas Grimshaw (1939–); Schlumberger HQ, Cambridge 19?, by Michael Hopkins (1935–); Millennium Wheel, London 2000, by Barfield Marks; Media Centre, Lord's, London 2000, by Future Systems.

132 Buildings by Mario Botta (1943–), Aldo Rossi (1931–), Jean Nouvel (1945–), Richard Meier (1934–) and James Stirling (1926–?)

133 Guggenheim Musem, Bilbao 1999, by Frank Gehry (1929–).

135 Palace of Sargon, Khorsabad 722–705 BC.

136 Temple of Horus, Edfu 237 BC; Great Temple of Ammon, Karnak 1301 BC.

140 The Parthenon, Athens 447–432 BC.

141 Caryatid from the Erectheum, Athens 421–405 BC; Temple of Empedocles, Selinius.

142 Royal Mosque, Isfahan 16th century; Taj Mahal, Agra 1648.

143 Ranakpur temple 143; Hindu temple, Neasden, London 19?.

144 Rockefeller and Vanderbilt residences 1881, by Richard Morris Hunt..

147 Reliance Building, Chicago 1894, and Monadnock Building, Chicago 1889, by Daniel Burnham (1846–1912) and John Root (1850–91); Carson Pirie Scott Store, Chicago 1901, and the Guaranty Building, Buffalo 1895, by Dankmar Adler (1844–1900) and Louis Sullivan (1856–1924).

148 American Radiator Building, New York 1924, by Raymond Hood (1881–1934).

149 Empire State Building, New York 1931, by Shreve, Lamb and Harman; Chrysler Building, New York 1928–30, by William van Alen; Rockefeller Center, New York 1933, by Associated Architects.

150 World Trade Center, New York 1966–73, by Minoru Yamasaki (1912–86); Seagram Building, New York 1954–58 by Mies van der Rohe; Lever House, New York 1952, by Gordon Bunshaft (1909–) of Skidmore, Owings & Merrill.

151 PPG Building, Pittsburg 1983, Republic Bank, Houston 1984, and the former AT&T Building, New York 1983, by Philip Johnson (1906–); Humana Building, Louisville, Kentucky 1986, by Michael Graves (1934–).

158–9 The Red House, Bexleyheath 1859, by Philip Webb (1831–1915).

160 Broadleys, Windermere 1878, by CFA Voysey (1857–1941).

160–61 Buildings by Frank Lloyd Wright (USA), Eero/Eliel Saarinen (Finland), Hendrik Berlage (the Netherlands), Peder Klint (Denmark), Charles Rennie Mackintosh Scotland, Antoine Pompe (Belgium), Joseph Olbrich (Austria), Peter Behrens (Germany).

162 Cow shed, Garkau Farm, Lubeck 1925, by Hugo Haring (1882–1958); Town Hall, Saynatsalo, Finland 1951, by Alvar Aalto (1898–1976); Leicester University Engineering Department 1963, by James Stirling (1926–92) and James Gowan (1923–).

163 Portcullis House, London 2001, by Michael Hopkins; Leicester University 1993 and Manchester University buildings date, by Short & Ford; Textile Faculty, Melbourne, by H2O Architects; Kindergarten, Stuttgart, by Gunther Benisch; Cottage in Wales, by David Lea.

169 Domes in Regent's Park, Venice, St Paul's, St Peter's, Florence; Dome of the Rock, Jerusalem; Dome of Discovery, 1951, by Ralph Tubbs etc; the Millennium Dome, London 2000, by Richard Rogers.

170 Yurt from North Kirghiz.

171 Set for the Rolling Stones *Steel Wheels* tour by Mark Fisher. Paintings of Mick Jagger by David Oxtoby.

173 Penguin pool 1933, by Berthold Lubetkin (1901–90); Aviary 1962, by Cedric Price and Frank Newby; Elephant and Rhino House 1965, by Sir Hugh Casson (1910–99).